J. Schüssler

The Oldenburg Horse

J. Schüssler

The Oldenburg Horse

ISBN/EAN: 9783845725147

Erscheinungsjahr: 2012

Erscheinungsort: Barsinghausen, Deutschland

Marktstraße 16 A, 30890 Barsinghausen.

www.unikum-verlag.de | info@unikum-verlag.de

Printed in Germany

Bei diesem Titel handelt es sich um den Nachdruck eines historischen, lange vergriffenen Buches. Da elektronische Druckvorlagen für diese Titel nicht existieren, musste auf alte Vorlagen zurückgegriffen werden. Hieraus zwangsläufig resultierende Qualitätsverluste bitten wir zu entschuldigen.

Covergestaltung meisterstudio ©

J. Schüssler

The Oldenburg Horse

The Oldenburg Horse

by

J. Schüssler
Secretary of the Society, Rodenkirchen.

Issued by
The Oldenburg Horse Breeders' Society
Rodenkirchen, Oldenburg.

With 1 Map, 1 Pedigree, 6 Formulars and 56 Illustrations.

Hannover.
M. & H. Schaper.
1914.

Photograph by Feltner & Mohaupt, Oldenburg.

Erbgraf, No. 1500, foaled 1900.
Sire: Ehrenberg, No. 1383; Dam: Namenschwester, No. 9229.
Erbgraf won 1902 Foal Prize, 1903 I. Advance-Money Prize, 1905 II. State Prize, 1906 at the Show of the German Agricultural Society in Berlin in the Karossier Class I. Prize and 1910 for excellent offspring I. State Prize.

From a picture by Professor Volkers, Düsseldorf.

The Oldenburg, No. 170, foaled 1848.
Sire: Ellwürder, No. 151.
Won 1851 I. State Prize.

Heil dir, o Oldenburg!
Heil deinen Farben!
Gott schütz' dein edles Ross,
Er segne deine Garben!
Heil deinem Fürsten, Heil,
Der treu dir zugewandt,
Der dich so gern beglückt,
O Vaterland!

v. Kobbe (1840).

Composed by the Grand Duchess Caecilie of Oldenburg.

First verse of the Oldenburg National Anthem.

From an oil painting by Professor Winter, Oldenburg.

Friedrich August, Grand Duke of Oldenburg.

1. Preface.

Owing to the ever increasing estimation in which the Oldenburg horse is held in the markets of the world, a large number of enquiries have been received concerning the manner in which it is bred and reared. For this reason, it seems justifiable ,to write a small book, compiled from original manuscripts and other authentic sources. (at the same time leaving out anything that does not fully bear on the subject in hand), to enable the horse breeders, who live outside our blue and red boundary-posts, to form some idea as to the origin of the race and also the cicumstances under which the Oldenburg horse lives; as well as to give the desired information, in condensed form, as to situation, kind of soil and agricultural conditions of the neighbourhood in which this horse is bred.

In the first place, the Oldenburg was the original breed that brought the German coach horse into notice abroad, unfortunately sometimes to the detriment of its name and also that of its breeders. Lately, however, it has been possible to alter this adverse opinion, especially since the Oldenburg "Karossier" (literally translated "State Coach Horse") has appeared at all the principal Shows at home and abroad and has gained universal admiration from breeders in general. The principal object of this little book is to extend the knowledge of the value and sphere of usefulness of our beloved "Oldenburgs" throughout the world.

Those however, who having read these pages and have become sufficiently interested to wish to visit us and see for themselves, may be assured that they will receive a "hearty welcome", not only from our officials but from all the breeders in the country.

Rodenkirchen in Oldenburg
February 1914.

The Author.

Contents.

From a picture by Professor Volkers, Düsseldorf.

2. *Geographical Position of the Breeding District and Conditions of Soil and Climate.*

On the left bank of the Lower Weser, below the old Hanse town of Bremen, there, where mighty ocean-going steamers pass by to connect the Old World with the New, lies the district in which for centuries the Oldenburg horse has been bred — the Oldenburg Weser Marsh. This, coupled with the JadeMarshes, which lie on the Jade Bay, situated to the west of the mouth of the Jade and named the Jeverland, consisting principally of marsh bounded by fen and "Geest"*) is the present home of the Oldenburg horse.

The breeding district is comprised of about two-thirds marsh and one-third moor and "Geest". All these

*) The "Geest" is so named in Oldenburg to distinguish it from the marsh proper; it lies rather higher, the soil is chiefly a diluvial deposit, and is not so fertile as that of the marshes.

The Grand Ducal Castle at Oldenburg.

different kinds of soil, however, are required to render horse breeding profitable, as they provide the necessary pasturage to ensure the quick development of the young animals. The marsh is alluvium; a clay that has been deposited by the rivers and the action of the sea and in which varying portions of sand have become mixed, rendering the soil heavier or lighter in places, according to the amount of sand contained therein. This tract of country is very fertile and has been gradually reclaimed from the sea after centuries of labour. High dykes, like huge fortress works, protect the marsh to the north and east from the inroads of the sea, which ever and anon makes renewed efforts to gain back the land which has been rescued from its clutches.

These dykes are from 9 to 20 feet in height above normal high water mark; they are 25 to 32 yards broad at the base, tapering to 2½ to 5 yards at the top. The strongest dykes are used to protect the marsh against the sea, they are often earthworks of considerable magnitude. There is a difference between the sea and the river-dykes. The seadykes are drawn round the Jeverland, the outer Jade and the Jade Bay to the mouth of the Weser; the river-dykes commence here and form one continuous line up the Weser and tributary rivers. The outer side of these dykes is built at a much more acute angle than the inside and at places, where the sea has considerable force, they are often strengthened by using concrete blocks to deaden the action of the waves.

After a picture from the Monograph "Weser Marsh Cattle".

Dam with sluice in the Weser Marsh (inside).

It is a heart-rending narrative, that which describes the fight of man against the elements: of high tides, of breaks in the dykes, through which thousands upon thousands of men and animals have lost their lives, whole villages and large tracts of fertile land being again engulfed by the ever devouring sea. God be praised, such catastrophies are a thing of the past and are likely to remain so, so far as the skill of man is capable of preventing them. By reason of a splendidly organised supervision of dykes, the inhabitants of the marshes can rejoice at their comparative great safety from the fury of the elements that the strengthened and heightened sea-walls have given them. Even the stranger, who lets his eye roam over our blessed Marshland in the glorious summer, can appreciate the love the inhabitants have for their hardly earned home; he understands that it has been worth while to combat for centuries against such odds to gain such a desirable end.

Standing on a dyke and looking inland, the marsh appears to the onlooker as one vast green plain of great fertility, studded here and there with well-built homesteads, with horses and cattle leisurely browsing or resting at will. The picture is bound to have a peculiar fascination for him who looks upon it for the first time. The advantage of grass-farming, in this neighbourhood, is at once apparent to the spectator, as he sees that the fields yield a good return for comparatively little labour; it is for this reason that arable farming has almost become obsolete. There are wide expanses in the Marshland that have not been under the plough within the memory of man, nearly all is laid down to pasture; this improves from year to year, owing to the care that is taken of it and affords excellent grazing ground for our young stock; indeed, we are much envied by our neighbours, who are less fortunately situated. The land outside the dykes provides abundance of good hay as it is often flooded by a high tide.

After a picture from the Monograph "Weser Marsh Cattle".

Dam with sluice in the Weser Marsh (outside).

The inland side of the marsh is nearly always bounded by fen which has been cultivated for ages past;

Photograph by Feilner & Mohaupt, Oldenburg.

Part of dam with sluice gates in the Weser Marsh (outside).

it is almost equal to the marsh in fertility and is used for the same purposes, namely, as pasture and meadow. Where marsh and fen meet and both kinds of soil can be used for the same agricultural purpose, they are often spoken of as "Fen-Marsh". Higher-lying moor land is used as arable, and where the soil is suitable peat for fuel is obtained. In places, the marsh bounds the more hilly "Geest"; here there are beautiful woods, also good pastures and fertile meadows.

A network of canals and smaller watercourses (sluice, boundary and draining ditches) is interwoven over the whole drainable extent of the country. In the Weser and the moor marshes, these ditches contain fresh water, so that nearly everywhere the stock is enabled to take drinking water from them. Drainage is carried out on the same principle as in Holland; owing to the flat nature of the country the fall is very slight, so that the ebb and flow of the Weser can be made use of when required.

The climate, on account of the proximity of the sea, is a damp one but is not subject to sharp changes in temperature; it is therefore well suited for stock-rearing. In spring and autumn there are often fogs, a heavily clouded sky and biting winds are frequent; on the other hand it is not too warm in summer and severe cold occurs but seldom in winter and then only for a short period. Our farmers can therefore nearly always reckon on an average pasturing season of about seven months, from May to November.

3. Characteristics of the Coach Horse and a General Survey of the Breed.

The Oldenburg is a strong heavy carriage horse (Karossier) which is at once shown by the following description; it has a muscular and symmetrical body with good neck, is placed on strong sinewy legs with plenty of bone and has a high energetic action. The colouring is brown, dark brown or black, nearly always a whole-colour with very few markings; there are also chestnuts and greys, these latter are, howe er, very scarce and are never used as stallions.

The Oldenburg has a robust constitution. He has to thank his upbringing for his hardy character, as he was reared in the open from earliest spring till late in the autumn and has to stand the various climatic changes that occur in the vicinity of the North Sea. He has one particular advantage over all other breeds, in that he comes earlier to maturity than they do.

The measurements and weights of Oldenburg mares and fillies, exhibited at the Shows of the German Agricultural Society, have been taken by the late Professor Dr. S. von Nathasius, Jena, who was kind enough to place them at our disposal; they indicate the early development of the Oldenburg Karossiers. We are pleased to be able to give our readers the benefit of these researches.

	Older Mares				Three-year-old-fillies			
	Weight			Shank or Cannon-bone measurements	Weight			Shank or Cannon-bone measurements
	cwt.	qr.	lbs.	in.	cwt.	qr.	lbs.	in.
1.	11	2	13	8 5/8	12	2	13	8 1/2
2.	12	2	11	8 1/4	12	2	11	8 1/2
3.	12	2	11	8 5/8	12	2	11	8 1/8
4.	12	1	1	8 5/8	12	0	23	8 1/2
5.	12	3	12	8 3/8	13	3	3	8 5/8
6.	12	1	22	8 5/8	12	2	24	8 3/8
7.	12	2	24	8 1/2	13	0	5	8 5/8
8	12	2	9	8 1/2	13	1	7	8 5/8
9.	12	2	9	8 1/2	13	0	21	8 3/8
10.	12	3	27	8 1/2	12	3	16	8 1/8
	125	0	27	85 1/8	127	3	2	84 1/8
Average	12	2	3	8 1/2	12	3	3	8 1/2 **nearly. (2/5 in.)**

The latest measurements supplied by Professor von Nathusius compare the difference between 21 three-year-old and 20 two-year-old fillies:

Photograph by Feilner & Mohaupt, Oldenburg.

Marsh Farm House and Buildings New Style.

Marsh Farm House and Buildings Old Style.

	3-year-old fillies	2-year-old fillies
Height	161.9 c.m.*)	159.3 c m.
Height at croup	161.7 „	159.4 „
Length of leg	85.9 „	87.0 „
Depth of breast	75.9 „	72 3 „
Girth	198.3 „	188.1 „
Breadth of breast	45.7 „	43.7 „
Breadth at croup	59.0 „	55 5 „
Circumference of shank or cannon-bone	21.2 „	20.8 „
Length of body	167.9 „	162.1 „
	cwt. qr. lbs.	cwt. qr. lbs.
Weight	12 1 0	10 3 13

The average height of 14 three-year-old colts chosen for service in 1910 was a little over $16^1/_8$ hands (1.68 cm.), cannon-bone measurement $9^3/_8$ in (23½ cm).

The Oldenburg has been bred almost entirely by small farmers since time immemorial, they usually have only two brood mares as the farms are not of sufficient size to allow of more being kept. The stallions also are in private ownership, there are no State or other Stud farms in Oldenburg. The mares are sent to the horse between March and the end of June. The fee is from £ 1. 10. 0 to £ 5.

On an average the stallion covers from 120—130 mares, the best stallions are, of course, very much in request. Notwithstanding the heavy work required of them, they are good stock-getters, some 75% of the mares remaining in foal. When the season is over, the stallions are sent to grass and remain there till the end of September or beginning of October if the weather is suitable. The brood mares, even when at work on the farm, are kept at pasture; if the work is heavy they are given some corn in addition. Foals stay at grass the whole summer until late autumn, the young horses are put to light work when they are two years of age. They are very tractable and let themselves be easily handled, if one takes ordinary precautions at first, they cannot be said to have any vice. When three years old they are put to all kinds of work and are then also used for breeding purposes.

Owing to the conditions of soil and weather during the winter, the horses come in for a good deal of

*) As the measurements vary so little, in some instances, they are given in centimeters for the sake of easier comparison, if reduced to inches complicating fractions would have to be used. A hand is roughly 10¼ centimeters.

rest; it is not infrequent that horses that have been constantly at work. are then. for weeks together, kept entirely in the stable, but this does not have a derogatory effect on their health, as would certainly be the case with an ordinary cart horse. The young animals are mostly kept in boxes during the winter. In districts where straw is not easily obtainable, moss litter (also called peat-litter) is now used and provides a splendid substitute. This is either bought direct from the factory in bales, or where the farmers have turf bogs of their own it is carted from thence, they also get their peat fuel from the same place. The litter is either torn asunder by machinery or is trodden to pieces by the horses themselves.

The Oldenburg horse is a good doer and is nearly always an excellent, though rather small feeder; the winter rations are comprised chiefly of well saved hay and oats. The older horses get, on an average, daily about 7 lbs. oats and as much hay, sometimes a little straw, as they care to eat; the younger horses 9—11 lbs oats, plenty of hay and a few mangels, the latter especially for the first few weeks after they have been brought in from grass. The brood mares, particularly at the latter part of their time, are exercised freely or put to light work, when near foaling they are watched day and night. In some districts the following custom holds good at night; a girth, to which a thin rope is attached, is buckled round the mare, the rope is passed through a block fixed in the ceiling, then taken and laid across the groom's bed; a rolled up horse cloth is tied to the further end of the rope, so that if the mare lies down, which seldom happens shortly before foaling, the groom is at once aroused. Some days after the birth of the foal if the weather is favourable, both mare and foal are put out to grass; at first they are stabled at night, but as soon as the foal is strong enough they are turned out for good. Foals that have been sold are usually weaned at four months, the others remain with the dam 5—7 months; they are then separated from her and the mare returns to her work on the farm.

By Court Photographer F. N. Schwartz, Berlin.

Four-in-Hand, three-year-old Oldenburg Colts.
Won I. Prize at the Show of the German Agricultural Society at Halle.

4. *A Special Account of the Various Kinds of Blood Used for the Consolidation of the Oldenburg Horse.*

The Oldenburg carriage horse has resulted from a cross of thoroughbred and half-bred stallions of the "Karossier" class, with typical Oldenburg mares, — it is seldom that an ideal has been so well thought out and carried with such zeal to perfection, as has been the case with the breeding of the Oldenburg horse, hence the uniform type that exists. The best of our horses have for their origin the "Stäveschen Stallion", but one must not forget that this horse had a splendid foundation for the furtherance of the breed in the mares then existing and also that the State Selecting Commission of those days was very strict in their choice of the animals that were to be used for stud purposes. To what blood the mares, at that time, owed their origin we have unfortunately no chance of determining as nearly all the pedigrees and descriptions of the mares were destroyed by a fire that took place at the Castle of Varel in 1757 where the stud documents were kept. At any rate, the horses of those days were of the heavy coach horse type, for the Oldenburg historian von Halem, writing of the times of Count Anton Günther (1603—1667) says: "The Oldenburg horses were prized by princes and potentates for their size, beauty and strength".

Photograph by Feilner & Mohaupt, Oldenburg.

Farm House and Buildings in Jeverland (old style).

The beforementioned stallion foaled in England in 1806, was in all probability a half-bred; he was bought at Brunswick in 1820 from the horse-dealers Stäve and Brandes after having been shown to the

Selecting Committee and approved of. The horse was, according to the protocol taken at the time, 12—18 years old, 11½ "Quartier" (about 16.3¾ hands) high, chestnut brown with star, "the build, shape, bone and muscles of the stallion were found to be of exceptionally fine proportions". He was only used for three years in the breeding district. The "Stäveschen Stallion" was the sire of "Neptun" foaled 1821 and of "Thorador" foaled 1823, it was these two stallions that became the sires of the most noted progeny. "Neptun" was the sire of "Alte Martensche Stallion" foaled 1835, he was used for 11 years in the district and produced most excellent results, in the last five years of his time he still was able to serve 200 mares, on an average, yearly, 80% of which remained in foal. The best horse sired by "Alte Martensche Stallion" was "Landessohn" out of the prize mare "Die Glückliche" (The Happy One). "Landessohn" became the sire of 35 stallions that were afterwards chosen by the Selecting Committee; of these the prize horses "Darius", "Orest", "Young Landessohn", "Der Gewaltige", "Albinus" and "Dettmers Landessohn" were the most noted. "Thorador", the other son of the "Stäveschen" sired the prize-winning stallion "Hubertus", who became the sire of "Alcibiades" and "Herodot" and grandsire of "Romulus", these three stallions did particularly good service to the breed. Another English horse, imported by the Grand Ducal Stud at Oldenburg, "Astonishment", stood from the year 1842 onwards. He was the sire of the prize-winning stallion "Der Noble" who was most successful, very many prize-winning animals being descended from him. A third English horse, the thoroughbred "Sportsmann", sire "Flexible" out of "Juliana", sired "Young Sportsman", dam, the prize-winning mare "Valetta" and the "Ellen Sportsman" out of a mare belonging

Photograph by Feilner & Mohaupt, Oldenburg.

Farm House and Buildings in Jeverland (new style).

to the Grand Ducal Stud. Both these horses have become noted through their progeny and have done much good to the Oldenburgs, especially "Young Sportsman" through his sons "Jader" and "Phönix", the last named out of the prize-winning mare "Penelope", her sire was the English thoroughbred "Grand Falconer" g. sire "Merlin", g. dam "Active". "Grand Falconer" was kept for service by the Grand Ducal Stud at Oldenburg in the year 1840. In 1849 four Cleveland bay stallions were imported from England by U. Lübben-Golzwarderwurp. Of these four horses the "Duke of Cleveland", sire "Magistrate", dam mare by "Conqueror" and the "Luks All", sire "Präsident", out of a mare by "Goldpipin" were the most noted. Of all the prize-winning sons of the "Duke of Cleveland", the "Young Duke of Cleveland", dam a mare by "Traber" whose dam was a Hanoverian mare, excelled his brothers "Ajax", "Mozart" and "Garibaldi" by the excellence of his offspring.

His best known son was "Kimme". He was the sire of 36 selected stallions and 40 prize-winning mares, besides a number of other excellent horses; this stamps him as the best sire of this line. "Kimme's" best sons were "Admiral", "Arminius", "Stedinger", "Mongole", "Armin", "Cyrus", "Secundus" and "Comet". His dam was out of the prize mare "Amanda", a daughter of the above-mentioned "Alcibiades". "Luks All" also much improved the breed through his son "Blücher" and grandson "Fürst Bismarck" by "Blücher". Another new strain was introduced in 1849 by "Menkes Senner", a son of the English thoroughbred "Brother to Rostrup", his dam was a good mare of the Senne Stud. This horse was foaled at "Lopshorn", a place belonging to the Senne Stud, his son "Martens Senner" was sire of the prize-winning stallions "Nelson" and "Nathan".

Photograph by Feilner & Mohaupt, Oldenburg.

Farm House and Buildings in the Moor-Marsh (old style).

After this no more thoroughbreds or half-breds of note were imported from England, the reason being that

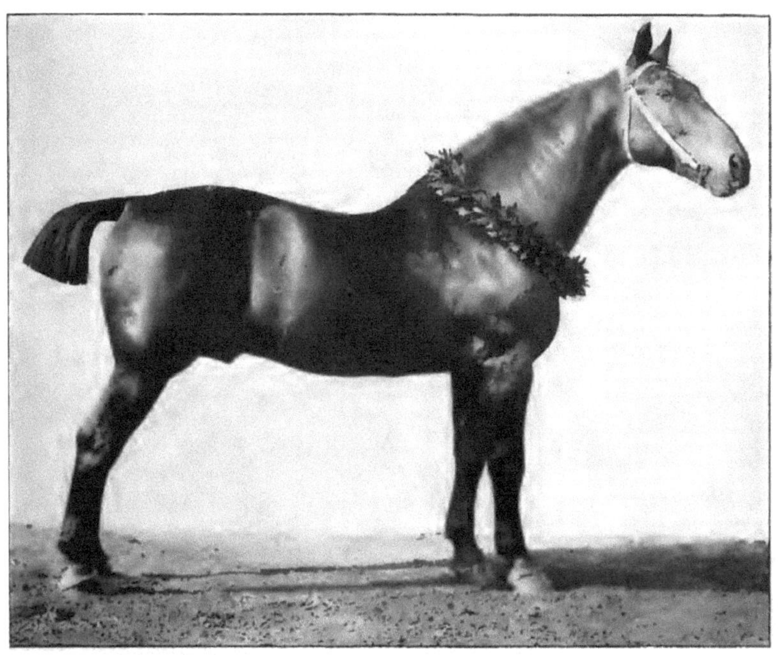

Photograph by Feilner & Mohaupt, Oldenburg.

The 25 year old Stallion **"Emigrant"** with Laurel-Wreath.
No. 925. foaled 1875.
1879 won I. Advance-Money Prize and 1886 for his
excellent offspring I. State Prize.
From Official Records it can be proved that he served
3083 mares from 1879—1900 of which 2324 remained in foal to him.

the English horses were too high on the leg and fine in the bone to be of any further service in producing the kind of animal required by the Oldenburg breeders. Several heavy half-bred horses were now imported from Hanover, many of which helped to improve the breed considerably: of these "Carolus" afterwards named "Graf Wedel" foaled in 1862 was very prominent, his sire was "Young Boradil" a noted Hanover stallion, dam a Hanover mare. "Graf Wedel" was instrumental in consolidating the Oldenburgs to a very great extent. "Young Boradil" was the grandson of the thoroughbred "Herodot", "Graf Wedel" was the sire of 29 selected stallions and of many excellent mares, his best known offspring were the prize-winning stallions "Atlas", "Neuenbroker", "Othello", "Tancred" and "Grossfürst". The in 1867 selected half-bred stallion "Agamemnon", sire, the Hanover Stud horse "Jellachich" (sire "Defensive", thoroughbred), dam a mare from the Hanover Stud horse "Zernebog" (sire, "Jupiter", thoroughbred) became a great factor in the Oldenburg breeding district. He was in use for 17 years and was the sire of 46 selected stallions besides a large number of valuable mares. The names of the best of these 46 stallions were "Magnat", "Rynald", "Jago", "Ardo" and "Admiral", who in their turn also produced a large amount of valuable breeding material. It may almost be looked upon as a record that four of the above-mentioned sons of "Agamemnon" were also in use in the district for 17 years; "Magnat" was the father of 34 selected stallions amongst which can be named the prize-winning "Magyar", "Young Magnat", "Modin", "Waltram", and "Matador", who rendered excellent service to the breed.

In 1871 the horse "Normann", sire, "Introuvable", dam, "Séduisante" was imported from Normandy; he was used for 16 years and produced 12 chosen stallions of whom "Rubico" was of the most service to the breed. "Rubico's" dam was by "Fürst Bismarck", his sire "Blücher", by "Luks All" (English half-bred) out of a mare by "Landessohn"; on his grandmother's side, "Rubico" had "Nelson" blood i. e. from the Senne Stud, and again on his great-great-dam's side blood from "Luks All". "Rubico" was used for nine years in the district and 17 chosen horses were descended from him, amongst which were "Wittelsbacher" and the now so noted stallion "Ruthard", the pedigree of this animal is to be found in the pocket of cover. It is not to be doubted that the young stock that came from "Rubico" owed their excellence as much to the noble blood from his dam's side as to that from his sire's; it is also certain that no other of "Normann's" sons improved the breed so much as "Rubico" has done.

Up to the present time, "Ruthard" who is now 20 years old, has produced 18 stallions for use in the district, amongst which we name the best known one "Ehrenberg", foaled in 1896. He has been a prize-winner from a foal onwards and in 1906 received the Goverment prize as the best stockgetter; he is also the sire of 216 stud mares, 49 of which have received prizes given by the State. "Ruthard" has also to thank his dam's strain of blood, which goes back seven times to thoroughbred, (see "Ruthard's" pedigree), for his success as a sire. The last, but not least important change of blood was introduced through "Emigrant" sired by a son of the Hanoverian Stud horse "Nord" out of a Hanoverian mare by the Hanoverian Stud horse "Consul", (sire, "Rostrums Bruder", a thoroughbred), a deeply built, heavy stallion of real "Karossier" type and action; he was imported in 1879 and was used for 21 years in the breeding district. When paired with mares from "Agamemnon" and "Graf Wedel" this horse was particularly successful in his progeny, whether fillies or colts; no less than 49 selected stallions are his sons and 50 of his daughters have been in receipt of prizes given by the State, while even in 1884, out of "Goldperle" by "Kimme"; "Eggi" was the father of the prize-winning "Enno" foaled in 1885, out of a mare by "Agamemnon". "Isenhard" was used for 9 and "Enno" 15 years in the district. Both stallions had excellent offspring which are being used at

From a picture by Professor Volkers, Düsseldorf.

Prize Stallion, **The Noble**, No. 145, foaled 1844.

Sire: Astonishment, Nr. 117, Dam: An Oldenburg mare.

Won 1848 a II. and 1852 a III. State Prize.

at the present time his daughters are much sought after for Stud purposes. The most noted sons of "Emigrant" were the prize-winning stallions "Eberhard", "Eggi", "Edgar", "Erwin" and "Congo". "Eberhard" sired the prize stallion "Isenhard" foaled stud to the present day. The most useful son of "Enno", for the improvement of the breed, was the prize stallion "Coco" foaled in 1891 out of the prize mare "Calma" by "Matador". "Coco" was used for 11 years; his most noted son the prize-winning "Elegant" foaled 1896, out of "Ludovika" by "Young Magnat" is still in use in the district, many good mares are descended from him, his most noted son up to the present being the prize horse "Elimar" foaled in 1902: this stallion has already done good service to the breed.

mares, 20 of which have received the State Premium. At the present moment "Ehrenberg" with 13 of his sons and 11 grandsons are standing in the district. As yet the best son of "Ehrenberg" is "Erbgraf" foaled in 1900; at the present time 13 of his sons have been selected for use

From a picture by Professor Volkers, Düsseldorf.

Landessohn, No. 157, foaled 1846.
Sire: Martens old Stallion, No. 107, Dam: Die Glückliche, No. 40.
Won 1850 a I. and 1856 a II. State Prize.

"Isenhard" was the grandsire of the above-mentioned "Ehrenberg" on his mother's side. The influence of "Ehrenberg" on the Oldenburg breed has been very marked, up to the present he is the father of 23 selected stallions and 165 chosen

in the district, five of which have been allotted prizes, namely "Edelbert", "Erbprinz", "Erlkönig", "Erbfürst" and "Eckstein". These are, in short, the principal strains that have been used to obtain the Oldenburg horse of the present day, a breed that, owing to its consolidation and truthfulness to type, has caused admiration at all Shows both at home and abroad; the honours that have been obtained at various Shows can be found in the chapter devoted to that purpose.

From the foregoing remarks it will be seen that "The Oldenburg" had its origin in an old race of horses peculiar to the country, which from time to time has been improved by the use of English thoroughbreds and well born half-breds, but the Oldenburg breeders have never committed the mistake, as has sometimes happened in other breeds, of allowing their animals to become too "fine" and notwithstanding the judicious use of "Blood" it can still be said that the old Marsh Horse has kept its place and has been of the greatest possible use in establishing the present breed. There is no doubt that the old Marsh Horse has been instrumental in preserving the strong legs, the sinewy muscles, the deep build, the hardy constitution, the even temperament and the early maturity of the race: it is to these

From a picture by Professor Volkers, Düsseldorf.

Young Landessohn, No. 199, foaled 1854.
Sire: Landessohn, No. 157, Dam: Madame, No. 226.
Won 1856 a I. and 1862 a II. State Prize.

excellent qualities that the Oldenburg owes its popularity and has established an ever increasing demand in the markets of the world. Other "warm" blooded breeds (in Germany, the distinction between "warm" and "cold" blooded horses is made, the former being all those used for really fast work, the latter being cart horses) have been gradually getting too fine and to a great extent, nervy; the Oldenburg on the contrary has kept his weight and is now acknowledged to be the heaviest "warm" blooded breed in the world; it is the endeavour of the breeders to stick to this record.

In no other breeding district, England scarcely excepted, have the breeders held so fast to the type of strong, muscular breeding animals of both sexes to produce a weighty carriage horse, as they have done in Oldenburg. It is owing to this principle that the Oldenburg, in spite of a little inbreeding to consolidate the race, has been able to preserve his excellent characteristics.

From a picture by Professor Volkers, Düsseldorf.

Young Duke of Cleveland, No. 200, foaled 1855.
Sire: Duke of Cleveland, No. 167, Dam: by Traber, No. 147.
Won 1859 a II. and 1863 a I. State Prize.

From a picture by Professor Volkers, Düsseldorf.

Magnat, No. 860, foaled 1874.
Sire: Agamemnon, No. 560, Dam: from Dettmers Landessohn, No. 351.
Won 1877 I. Advance-Money, 1878 II. State and 1882 for
his excellent Offspring a I. State Prize.

From a picture by Professor Volkers, Düsseldorf.

Selecting a Stallion in the Seventies.

Count von Wedel, Lieutenant-General, Chairman.

Master of Horse Rumpf, permanent Member.

5. The History of the Breed.

a) Notices regarding the Condition and Management of the Breed from Earliest Times to the Year 1820.*)

The first authentic information about the Oldenburg horse dates from the 15th. century. Even then, the chronicler Hamelmann speaks of "the beautiful horses of Oldenburg", also, as the Privy-Counsellor Hofmeister tells us in his work, "Horse Breeding in the Duchy of Oldenburg 1583 to 1584", that from State papers it appears that Count Johann XVI. made many gifts of horses in the years 1583 to 1589, (see appendix A), also that he had an extensive stud of these noble animals previous to 1583. From this and other parts of Hofmeister's writings, we may almost take it for granted that Johann XVI. was the first to introduce new strains for the improvement of the stud on his various farms; the other people in the country, however, were still conten-

Photograph by Feilner & Mohaupt, Oldenburg.

Aged Stallion (20 years) **Ruthard,** No. 1255, foaled 1890.
Sire: Rubico, No. 952, Dam: Grafin, No. 3652.
Won 1893 I. Advance-Money, 1894 II. State and 1900 for his excellent Offspring II. State Prize.

*) Partly taken from the work "The Oldenburg Carriage Horse" issued by the Society in 1902.

ted to keep to the original breed and that Count Anton Günther, the successor of Johann XVI., who was well known outside his own small Country, in which he reigned during the Thirty Years' War, was the one who strived to improve the breed in general outside his own stud. Count Anton Günther was without doubt the most successful breeder and connoisseur of horses in his time, and we have to thank him for the fact that the Oldenburg became known throughout Europe as a race apart. The native horse of that time was big, broad, strong boned and high on the leg, it enjoyed a good reputation and was much used to introduce fresh blood into other breeds.

Oldenburg horse breeding was at its best during the time of Count Anton Günther (1603—1667). He not only increased the number and general condition of stud farms on his own estates, but also interested himself in the improvement of the native breed. Thanks to the statesmanship of Count Anton Günther, he managed not only to keep Oldenburg free from invasion, by giving subsidies and horses to the armies of Tilly and Mannsfield during the Thirty Years' War, thus incidentally saving his own horses, but also prevented his country from being devastated at a time when the whole of Germany was almost ruined by the ravages of war, horse and cattle

Photograph by Fellner & Mohaupt, Oldenburg.

Ehrenberg, No. 1383, foaled 1896.
Sire: Ruthard, Nr. 1255, Dam: Giba, No. 1146.
Won 1897 and 1898 Foal, 1899 II. Advance-Money, 1901 III. State, and 1896 for his excellent Offspring I. State Prize.

breeding in Oldenburg suffered comparatively little harm.

Anton Günther, with his intimate knowledge of horse breeding and well-filled coffers, did not only confine himself to the buying up of breeding animals likely to suit his purpose, but recognised that it was all important to introduce the love of horses to his subjects. To this end, he stimulated the enthusiasm of the breeders in the right direction, teaching them how they should take care of their animals to obtain the best results. The young peasants were taught to ride, drive and groom their charges, not with the object only of their becoming helpers on his numerous stud farms, but that the youth of the country should gain an intimate knowledge of horse breeding and to awake in them an interest for the general good and well being of the breed at large.

In addition to this the people were allowed the use of the stallions at the stud farms and better mares were provided for them. To increase the sale of his horses. Anton Günther founded various markets or horse fairs where the animals were shown to the best advantage; he also made numerous presents to princes and potentates so that the fame of the Oldenburgs might become more widely known. (See appendix B and C.)

These measures had their due reward, especially the presents that were made in various high quarters, as where the horses were used at State functions they were seen by many people, some of whom were fired by the desire to possess like animals themselves. To give only a few examples: we know that the Emperor Leopold I., after his marriage in the year 1658, made his State entry into Vienna riding on a black Oldenburg charger and that the State Coach of the young Empress was drawn by six cream-coloured Oldenburg horses, the gift of Count Anton Günther.

With. Hoffmann, Dresden.

Collection of two and three-year-old Oldenburg Horses.
Won 1st and Champion Prize at the Show of the German Agricultural Society held at Düsseldorf in 1907.

A great connoisseur of a horse at that time was the Duke of Newcastle, who mentions meeting Queen Christine of Sweden at Antwerp. He says she had a number of rather poor looking Swedish saddle horses, but in addition to these eight large coach horses from the Count of Oldenburg's stud farms, "they were broad in the chest and loins, upstanding, with well formed heads and necks, cream coloured, with white tails and manes and were the best goers he had ever seen. She gave some like them to the King of Spain. verily a kingly present, worthy of both giver and receiver".

As the historian of Count Anton Günther, J. J. Winkelmann tells us, Count Aldenburg, who was staying in London in 1653, presented six beautiful dapple-grey horses to the Protector O. Cromwell, in his father's, Anton Günther's, name. In 1672 King Christian II. of Denmark founded the so-called Krodahl Stud near Esserum by importing the white stallion "Jungfrau" from Oldenburg. The horses from this stud gave great satisfaction, not only on account of their white colour but because they were the best bred, strongest and most hardy animals that were produced in Denmark.

It is worthy of remark, that in the 17th century conspicuous colours, beautiful manes and tails were highly prized; in the Danish Stud, horses of all colours were to be found, piebald, skewbald, cream coloured, pearl coloured and white were all represented at this period; amongst the Oldenburg, besides browns and blacks with black manes and tails, bright chestnuts with white manes and tails, dappled and pearl coloured horses*) were prevalent. The favourite charger of

*) Even at this period, in spite of the taste for showy animals, the chief aim of the breeders was directed to size, shape and good action in their horses.

The Grand Duke Friedrich August at a Premium Parade for Mares.

× The Grand Duke.

Photograph by Fellner & Mohaupt, Oldenburg.

Count Anton Günther, the grey stallion "Kranich", was far-famed, he had a wonderful mane and tail. The mane was 7 ells (4 yds. 10 in.) in length and is still shown in Oldenburg, the tail which was 9 ells long (5yds. 1 ft. 9 in.) is at Copenhagen.

We are unfortunately without reliable information as to the exact number of horses kept at Count Anton Günther's various stud farms, but from extracts made by Hofmeister we learn that 1432 horses were on his books on the 1st January 1664, of these at least 250 were used for schooling, riding and driving purposes, so that we should not be much out in guessing that the stud consisted of at least 1200 animals. A book written in Italian was published 1661, by someone who had evidently spent a long time at Anton Günther's Court, as he gives a description of the country and also of what went on at the former. Amongst other things, Hofmeister has translated the following passage. "Before all else, I must mention the number and quality of the horses kept by the Count at his numerous stud farms, situated in various parts of the country; they are something to see and admire. There are from 1000 to 1200 of the handsomest horses imaginable and more than 70 to 80 stallions from Naples, Spain, Turkey, Poland, Tartary and other lands all got together regardless of expense. One can say with truth, that no other prince or potentate in Europe possesses larger, more beautiful or more numerous horses and a greater variety of breeds than the Count; in addition to this the colourings are so remarkable, that I am sure that in no other place can such a choice or better horses be found."

Clemens Count von Wedel, Master-of-the-Horse, 1873/84. **Wilhelm Count von Wedel,** Lieutenant-General, 1834/72.

Chairmen of the Grand Ducal Selecting Committee from 1834/1884.

The same author also tells us that the Count possessed six coaches, with six horses to each, 100 excellent riding-school horses and 100 saddle horses for daily use. Finally, he says that the land is fairly fertile with a large amount of good pasture, where so many cattle and horses are at grass that he is sure no country of the like size can equal it and adds, in the quaint language

Ummo Lübben, Golzwarderwurp.

Sat for a number of years on the Grand Ducal Selecting Committee.

of that time, that the inhabitants who breed cattle and horses in this country "feel themselves satisfied and in comfortable circumstances". He mentions that 5000 horses were bought yearly at the best markets in Oldenburg, during the months of June and July: these were sent to Flanders, France, Italy and other countries. This shows that horse-breeding was carried on as extensively by the inhabitants of Oldenburg then, as it is now.

At the death of Anton Günther some of the stud farms were unfortunately broken up. This was caused in a measure by the counties of Oldenburg and Delmenhorst becoming Provinces of Denmark for a hundred years and the Jeverland became subject to the Principality of Anhalt-Zerbst for nearly as long a period. The Danish Royal Family had to take the highest interest in European affairs and could therefore not afford to pay the same attention to horse breeding as the late Count. It was indeed lucky that the interest in horse-breeding which Anton Günther had awakened in the people during his more than sixty years' reign, did not allow it to fall into decay; for, in spite of Oldenburg having to contribute to the maintenance of the French troops in the year 1679 in the war with Denmark, and also owing to the dreadful inundations in 1717 and 1721, the good name of the Oldenburg horse almost held its own in foreign countries, as we learn from a book entitled "The Riding School", issued in 1746 by Baron Eisenberg, as follows: "Of all the under-mentioned breeds of horses, the Dutch, Friesland, Holstein, Jutland, Swedish etc. etc., the Oldenburgs are the best."

From regulations concerning the choice of stallions etc., issued by the Ducal Chamber in 1784, we know that the number of horses in Oldenburg must have been considerable at that time. Sir Walter

Heinrich Martens, Moorsee.

Sat for a number of years on the Grand Ducal Selecting Committee.

Gilbey, the well-known hackney breeder, in his book "The Harness Horse", says, "Supposing that a long line of ancestors is any criterion for the purity and quality of blood in horses, as it is taken to be in man, then the hackneys should be better than the thoroughbreds owing to their long pedigrees." We are then also justified in taking this to apply equally to the Oldenburgs: the pedigrees of these date back not only to the beginning of the 18th century, as some of those of the hackney families do, but to a much remoter period, namely that of Count Anton Günther in 1603; for though it is not possible to give the pedigrees on paper from that date onward, owing to the Stud Book being of later formation, we know that horse-breeding was carried on then on almost the same lines as it is now.

The State did not again begin to take an interest in horse-breeding till 1780; unfortunately the measures then instituted did not have a lasting effect and came to an end in 1793, as also did others proposed by the Duke Fredrich August for the improvement of the breed, but the regulations then made formed the basis of the rules established in 1820, and still in force, regarding the choice of and prizes to be given to stallions, also the lowest price that was to be paid for service fees.

Not only the choice of suitable stallions was settled at this time but also the abuse that then existed of using two-year-old colts for breeding purposes was gone into and was strictly forbidden. This rule raised a storm in some quarters; as a result the Duke rescinded it and requested his Chamber of Agriculture to draw up new regulations under the heading of "Ground lines of the regulations for the State improvement of horse-breeding in Oldenburg". The Duke Friedrich August died in 1785: this event coupled with the French Revolution and the uncertainty that existed in consequence, was the cause that no further improvements were made at that time. It was nearly 20 years after that the State again began to take up the interests of horse-breeding. Were it not for

Photograph by Feilner & Mohaupt, Oldenburg

Market Place and Stables in Rodenkirchen i. O.

the fertility of the soil and the interest the breeders took in their horses, owing to their inherited love of their animals, the situation would have been much worse. As it was, when the State again, in 1819, bethought itself to take up the improvements suggested by the late Duke Friedrich August, it found that there were still the goodly number of 9000 mares left in the country suitable for breeding purposes.

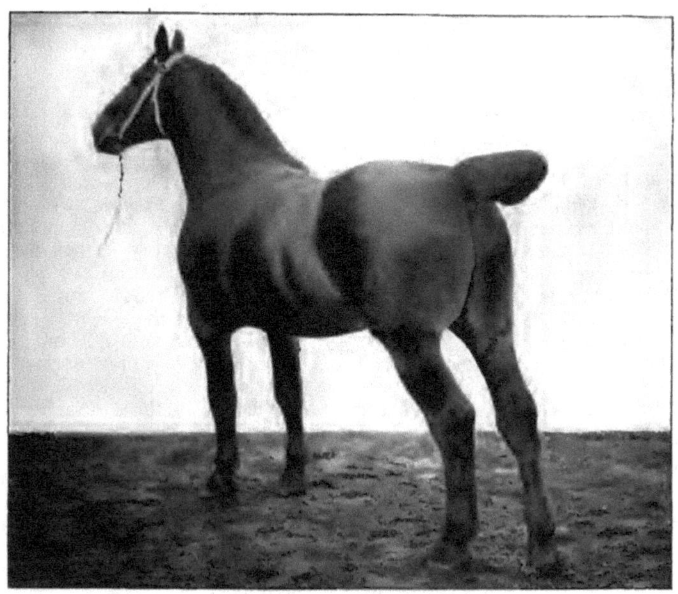

Photograph by Feilner & Mohaupt, Oldenburg.

Gisbert, No. 1523, foaled 1901.
Sire: Gilbert, No. 1405, Dam: Edelgart, No. 9967.
Won 1906 a III. State Prize.

b) Measures taken to promote the improvement of Oldenburg Horse-breeding from the year 1820 to the time New Regulations ware passed in 1897.

At the end of the year 1819 the State passed a Statute which had for its object the placing of our horse breeding on a wider and more prosperous basis and was therefore the landmark, in the history of the Oldenburg horse, from which our present success dates. It was as follows:

1. That all stallions, used on mares not belonging to the owner of the stallion, must be at least three years of age and of tried and acknowledged capability.
2. That the best stallions should receive a premium of 100 gold thalers (about £ 15).

3. That the lowest service fee be fixed at 1½ gold thalers (about 4/6).

The stallions for the year 1820 were at once selected and Committees were formed of 3 permanent and 7 members elected from the breeders in the district, one Committee for the northern and the other for the southern division of the country, to choose the stallions allowed to serve and to receive premiums in each successive year.

It was very soon found that this system was too cumbersome to work well. It was therefore decided in 1823 that the Selecting Committee should consist of the 3 permanent and 2 elected members for each division of the country, but that the horses to receive the premiums were to be chosen by the full Committee of 10 members. We find it was the endeavour of the members of the northern division to keep the breed true to the heavy coaching type, while in the southern division lighter horses were often taken. The authority and scope of these Committees extended considerably in the course of time, as may be seen from the regulations in force in 1861.

1. To choose suitable horses for service; also to decide all disputes arising in case of a stallion that had once been chosen being condemned for further use.
2. To settle which stallions and mares were to receive the premiums.
3. To look after the Stud Books.
4. To bring all suggestions, made by third persons as to the improvement of horse-beeding, as well as their own, under the direct notice of the Government.

The new regulations also made it compulsory for the owners of stallions to keep a list of all mares served and with what results, so that it could be seen at a glance which horses were most sought after by the breeders and which were most serviceable to the breed in general. This regulation still continues in force and has proved to be most useful in helping the various Breeding Societies when entering their animals in the Stud Book. These same new regulations divided the country into three districts, the Marsh district, the Middle or mixed soil district and the "Geest" district. These districts elected members to serve on the Committees with the three permanent members, the Marsh district elected three, the others two apiece. The Commissioners, even more than they had ever done before, kept to the type of the heavy coach horse in the Marsh and Mixed districts, but in the "Geest", chiefly in the so-called Münsterland, they bred a carriage horse of medium weight.

The work, in these decades, was carried on by persons of great influence who possessed a thorough knowledge of the subject in hand and the good they accomplished, as Committee men, for the improvement of the Oldenburg breed, ought not to be forgotten. Most of them have passed away: we wish here to keep their memory green, not only in the present but also future generations, to show our thankfulness for what they have done. In the first place we mention two Counts von Wedel, Oldenburg, father and son; then the Master-of-the-Horse Rumpf, Oldenburg, the Chief Master-of Horse, General von Schneben, Oldenburg; and lastly the breeders H. Martens, Moorsee, Ummo Lübben, Golzwarderwurp, Günther Lüken, Rhaude, Hinrich Lüershen, Oldenbrok. The chief merit of these men lay in the fact that they resolutely stuck to the original type of the Oldenburg horse when making choice of the stallions for use in their districts and did not allow themselves to be influenced, in any way, by modern ideas, such as crossing with thoroughbred or half-bred without considering the effect it would have on the future of the breed: in fact, we may say it was these men who saved our treasured

Oldenburg Premium Brand.

heavy coach horse from degeneration and decay. — The giving of premiums to the best selected stallions since 1820 and to mares from 1840, proved itself to be of great benefit in the improvement of the breed. At the beginning, these prizes only amounted to 50—100 gold thalers (£7. 10. 0 to £ 15. 0. 0) for stallions and from 50—75 gold thalers (£ 7. 10. 0 to £ 11. 5. 0) for the best mares. As, however, the value of the horses increased, and the prize horses, notwithstanding the fact that the premiums had then to be paid back to the State, were sold to go abroad, the premiums were raised considerably. Since the year 1876 the premiums have been as follows: in the Marsh and Middle districts, for stallions which have proved themselves of value for breeding purposes, **£ 90, £ 75 and £ 60** and advance-money for young likely looking colts £ 37. 10. 0 and £ 30. These figures still hold good in the northern district. **£ 20, £ 15** and **£ 10** were paid to keep selected mares.

The rules, regarding the registration of horses, in the Regulations of 1861, were at first not well received; as a consequence very few applications for entering the animals were sought for. In 1886, however, the Ministry of State issued "new directions for the management of the pedigree registers"; the result was that more interest was aroused and a few more animals were entered. In the above-mentioned Regulations, it was made a s i n e q u â n o n that only animals free from hereditary faults could be entered. All horses entered must be at least three years old and have a clean sheet of their own to show that their parentage,

Oldenburg Stud-Book Brand.

on both sides was true to the type of this breed. Horses of other descent were also accepted when it could be shown, that throught their offspring they were capable of improving the Oldenburgs. Although the new Regulations were a step in the right direction, they only served to ensure the registration of really choice animals. It was not a register that showed the blood of all the animals used for breeding purposes and without which all rational breeding is illusory. On account of the fast growing export of Oldenburg horses to the United States, this Registration of animals did not prove sufficient, as the American Customs required a pedigree going back to the third generation, to allow horses to be imported free of duty, otherwise a duty of 25% on the price paid for the horses was imposed. Under such circumstances, the Oldenburg horse-breeders were at a great disadvantage, in spite of the fact that their horses had been bred true to type during a couple of centuries and the sires carefully selected, as compared with other world wide known breeders who had been careful to keep their pedigrees, including those of the mares, from the commencement of their efforts in horse breeding.

It is therefore plain that no other means could help the Oldenburg breeders better than the immediate revision of the pedigrees of their animals, to try to regain the ground lost in the years of inactivity, by endeavouring, as far as possible, to utilise the material on hand relating to the descent of the stallions and mares known to have been used in the formation of the breed and arrange it in consecutive order. The well-known breeder, Ed. Lübben Sürwürden, undertook this task on his own responsibility, and by publishing the first volume of the Oldenburg Stud Book accomplished this end with brilliant success. He took, for the foundation of his work, the official papers of the Grand-ducal Selecting Committee that was formed in 1820 and for information before this date, he made use of any books or papers that could be found bearing on his subject, but more especially quoted from the book entitled "Horse Breeding in the Duchy of Oldenburg" written by Privy-Counsellor Hofmeister. A great many native horses had officially recognised pedigrees long before the Selecting Regulations of 1820 were passed and on this account they had undoubted advantage over horses of many other breeds. There was no well ordered register, however, where the pedigrees could be followed easily by the use of numbers and names. The compiler of the Stud Book held this to be essential and entered all pedigrees, given in official documents, after this fashion, thus considerably increasing the scope of his work. From 1820—1860 all stallions that had received premiums, all selected Stud horses, and sires whose offspring had been selected and from 1860 onward all premium and selected mares and their progeny were entered. The pedigrees of these horses, with numbers and names attached, formed the first volume of the Oldenburg Stud Book. It was now possible to obtain reliable pedigrees for a large number of Oldenburg horses.

Lübben had also another object in view in founding the Stud Book: owing to the ever-increasing use of other breeds of horses for various employments, from which even Oldenburg was not exempted; the danger existed, that they might be used for breeding purposes and the old native breed thus become contaminated from other sources and not kept pure. This evil was hindered by the Stud Book, because it had to be proved conclusively that every animal entered was of pure Oldenburg blood on both

Grey Oldenburg Stallion (after Ridinger) 1760.

sides; this enabled the careful breeder to mate his stock with a full knowledge of their antecedents. It also confirmed the breeder's axiom that to mate animals from sight only, without knowing their history, was to court disaster and might easily become dangerous to the future welfare of the breed.

After a picture by Professor Volkers, Düsseldorf.

Erra II., No. 9628, foaled 1897.
Sire: Ruthard, No. 1255, Dam: Erra, No. 3046.
Won II. State Prize. International Show Paris 1900, I. Prize and Gold Medal and Champion Prize and large Gold Medal.
Sold to Sir Walter Gilbey, Elsenham Hall, Essex, England.

The first edition of the Stud Book, which appeared in 1891, was an up to-date work and showed the pedigrees to suitable advantage. A large number of Oldenburg breeders saw the force of Lübben's ideas and under his guidance, within a year, no less than 350 of them formed an association entitled "Oldenburg Coach Horse Breeders' Association". This Association undertook the further editions of the Stud Book and had the satisfaction, amongst other things, of finding it accepted by the Government at Washington. As a result, horses could now be exported duty free to America, if the pedigrees could be certified as correct through the officials of the Oldenburg Stud Book. This induced a still larger number of breeders to join the Association; for the duty that had formerly to be paid to the United States now, or at least the greater part of it, fell to their share.

During the time that the Stud Book was being created by private initiative, the before-mentioned State "Pedigree Register" had been undergoing improvement and an enlargement of the work taken in hand; the result was, that a large number of horses were entered in both the Oldenburg "Stud Book" and the State "Pedigree Register". This led to dire confusion, as the numbers and names were not uniform in each book, uninitiated persons could, therefore, not come to a clear understanding of the pedigrees of Oldenburg horses.

On this account it became imperative to have only one book for registration. To this end, the "Oldenburg Coach Horse Breeders' Association" requested the Government in 1892 to take over the Stud Book and put it in the place of their own, not too perfect, "Pedigree Register". It was not till 1897, however, that the State gave up their own Register and accepted the Stud Book of the "Oldenburg Coach Horse Breeders' Association", thus introducing a new era with an up-to-date Stud Book managed by the State.

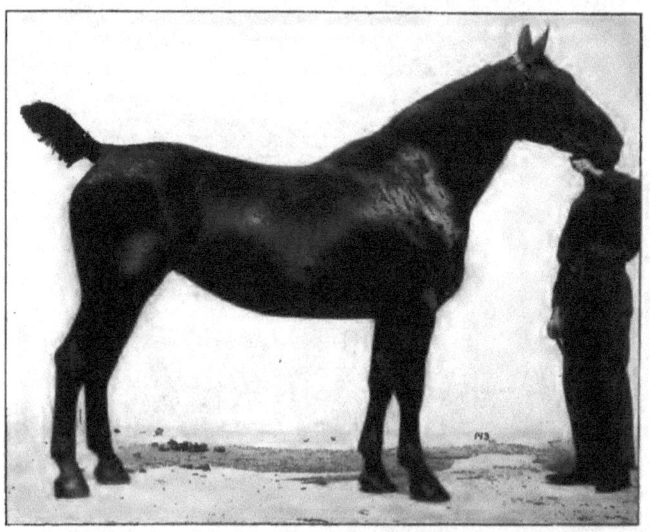

Photograph by Court-photographer, F. A. Schwartz, Berlin.

Three-year-old filly **Osterblume**, No. 12683, foaled 1902.
Sire: Elegant, No. 1387, Dam: Olympia II., No. 8623.
Won Ia and Champion Prize at the Show of the German Agricultural Society held at Munich.
Osterblume was sold to the Bavarian Royal Stud.

c) Horse Breeding after the New Regulations of 1897 and Prospects for the Future.

The new Regulations not only settled the question as to how the pedigrees were to be entered in the Stud Book in future, but many of the older laws were revised and others enacted. The principal changes were as follows:

1. Dividing the Duchy into two districts.
2. Another form of electing the Selecting Committee.
3. Formation of two independent Breeders' Associations.
4. The issue of two Stud Books.

8 1 2 3 4 5 6 7

Photograph by J. Delton, Bois de Boulogne.

1. Ahsbahs, Elmshorn, Holstein. 2. Lübben, Sürwürden, Oldenburg. 3. Runge, Insterburg, East Prussia. 4. Stöckel, Insterburg, East Prussia. 5. Kosegarten, Schleswig. 6. Wegener, Norden, East Friesland. 7. von Drahten, Elmshorn, Holstein, Representative of the Central Committee. 8. Willrath, Norden, East Friesland.

Representatives of the German Horse Breeding Districts at the International Show at Paris, 1900.

5. The introduction of two brandmarks for all horses entered in the Stud Books and also for horses and foals, where notice had been given of entry, when they became the right age.
6. Premiums to be given to colt and filly foals.

has been carried on with such marvellous success, the Marsh, the Middle and the adjoining parts of the "Geest" — i. e. the northern half of the Duchy — has been allotted to this breed and for the breeders in this neighbourhood "The Society of Breeders of the Oldenburg Heavy

6 4 7 2 1 3 8 5

Photograph by Feilner & Mohaupt, Oldenburg.

1. Master of the Horse von Wenckstern, Oldenburg, Chairman. 2. Agricultural Counsellor Lohe, Seedeich, 1st permanent member. 3. Agricultural Counsellor Joh. Heinrichs, Oldenburg, 2nd permanent member. 4. G. Meyer, Oldenburg, elected member. 5. H. Thöle, Butzhausen, elected member. 6. G. Mennen, Bübbens, elected member. 7. Veterinary Dr. Greve, Oldenburg, Head Veterinary. 8. Recorder Runge, Oldenburg.

Photograph of the Grand Ducal Selecting Committee for Oldenburg in the year 1907.

The division of the Duchy into two districts, instead of three, as had been the case since 1861 (see above) was officially settled, as had long been determined by the nature of the soil and climatic conditions, by setting the boundary there, where the varied aims of the breeders almost meet. The district, in which since olden times the breeding of the heavy Oldenburg coach horse Coach Horse" has been established. The law has thus given the Oldenburg horse breeders the right to look after their own interests and the Council in consequence has become the officially recognised head in matters relating to horse breeding. The breeders of the medium heavy carraige horse live in the southern portion of the Duchy and called their Association "South

Secretary of the Society J. Schüssler, Rodenkirchen. E. Tantzen, Stollhamm. D. Wilken, Borgstede.

Agricultural Counsellor Schroeder, Nordermoor, Vice-Chairman. Agricultural Counsellor Lübben, Sürwürden, Chairman. H. Habben, Quanens.

The Council of the Oldenburg Heavy Coach Horse Society.

Oldenburg Horse Breeders' Society". Both Societies now had separate Selecting Committees, their own system of allotting premiums and their own Stud Book. In consequence of these regulations, the Selecting Committee consisted of three permanent members appointed by the State and three members of the Society are chosen from amongst themselves, but have to be approved of by the State. The Commission, besides selecting horses, also decides which stallions, mares and foals are to receive premiums and acts as judge in the Riding and Driving Competitions and awards prizes. It is consulted on all questions relating to horse breeding by the Ministry of State and when required give its opinion.

The regulations also allow the Selecting Committee to have all the progeny of the various stallions brought before them for inspection. Great use has been made of this right lately; it is a measure much approved of by the breeders, because the quality of the offspring must always be taken into consideration in determining the value of the parents for breeding purposes. The Selecting Commission is the acknowledged head of all things concerning horse breeding in Oldenburg. By having horses selected and allowing the use of these only, the State encroaches on the rights of breeders; but as studying the pedigree and looking at the offspring of the sire to be chosen, is the first thing a thoughtful breeder ought to do, he does not find that the far-reaching authority of the Selecting Committee presses unduly upon him.

Botho No. 1357. *Photograph by J. Delton, Bois de Boulogne.* Freibeuter No. 1522.

Group of the Societies' Representatives and Grooms at the International Show at Paris in 1900.

On the contrary, many of them think that the parents still living, as well as the brothers and sisters, ought to be mustered before a horse is permanently selected. The organisation, called into being by the Regulations Concerning Horse Breeding, "The Society of Breeders of the Oldenburg Heavy Coach Horse", is shortly as follows: every owner of a brood-mare entered in the Stud

Book is a member of the Society. Each circuit is represented by a chairman and three other members placed on their honour to do what is just and fair. The 37 chairmen are at the same time the Council to whom the management of the affairs of the Society are entrusted. The Council elects five of their members, who must be farmers as well as breeders, to look after all business matters of the Society, these men are also placed on their word of honour. The five selected members of the Council since its foundation are the following: Agricultural Counsellor Ed. Lübben, Sürwürden, Chairman; Agricultural-Counsellor Schroeder, Nordermoor, Vice-Chairman; the horsebreeders H. Habben, Quanens, E. Tantzen, Stollhamm and D. Wilken, Borgstede are members; and G. Köster, Ofen is the proxy in case one of the others is not able to be present at the meetings. The clerical work is undertaken by a secretary who is sworn in to keep the Stud Book properly and who is at the same time bookkeeper and clerk to the Society, his proper title being "Secretary of the Society". The expenses of the Society, if there is no help forthcoming from the State or other sources, are paid for by the entry of horses by members and in this wise; the owner of a horse given a premium by the State, pays four units, of a selected stallion three units, of a State premium mare two units and of a brood-mare one unit. Since the foundation of the Stud Book the unit for a brood-mare, on an average, has amounted to about four shillings.

Photograph by J. Delton Bois de Boulogne.

Pair of three-year-old Oldenburg Fillies.
Won I. Prize at a Driving Competition in 1909.

The objects of the Society are:

1. To propose persons, with a thorough knowledge of horse-flesh, to act on the Selecting Committee.
2. Keeping the Stud Book correctly.
3. To make suitable and useful suggestions for the improvement of the breed.
4. To improve the breeding material in the district, by finding out where particulary promising animals are, by giving premiums to the same and, if necessary, buying them up to ensure of their being kept in the country for further use.
5. All other useful measures to promote horse-breeding in the district, such as facilitating the sale of animals, developing external trade, holding of and sending to Horse Shows, management of riding and driving competitions, planning and building model stables and the furtherance of good shoeing and care of the hoof.

The regulations regarding the registration of horses are as follows:

As foundation, for the new registration of horses, which in the future is to be called "The Stud Book", and which is drawn up on nearly the same lines as the Oldenburg Stud Book, the Oldenburg Stud Book, Vols. I. and II. and the old Pedigree Register have been consulted. All mares in the breeding district, that were not entered in the Oldenburg Stud Book or the Pedigree Register or their progeny, had to be inspected; if they were suitable, true to type and blood, they were entered in the third volume of "The Stud Book", this third volume being a continuation of Vol. II. of the Oldenburg Stud Book.

The Regulations further determined that the progeny of a mare that was already registered in the Stud Book was in the first place to be entered on the same page as its dam; as soon as it was used for breeding purposes however, it was

Photograph by F. A. Schwartz, Berlin.

Oldenburg Four-in-Hand, foaled 1896 and 1897.
Won I. Prize at the Show of the German Agricultural Society at Hanover 1903.
The off leader Valda, No. 10109 won I. and Champion Prize in her Single Class.

entered on a page of its own without the necessity of having first to be mustered by the Selecting Committee. When we consider the wonderful uniformity of the Oldenburg horse, produced by over 100 years of careful breeding, we are gladdened by the thought that it was not deemed necessary for the mares to have to pass the Selecting Committee before being entered in the Stud Book; it was a well deserved tribute to the consistency of the Race as well as to the founders of the Oldenburg Stud Book.

Besides the 1600 stallions entered in the Pedigree Register, there were 8400 mares entered in the Oldenburg Stud Book, just after the compulsory mustering; the entries now number over 16.000. All the pedigrees and entry sheets are examined most carefully and fines imposed for any doubtful information contained therein; in some cases still harder punishments are inflicted by the Regulations. The entries are made in the Stud Book by the Secretary (on oath) and controlled by the Chairman of the circuit from which they are sent. The Chairman of each circuit has his own register, in which all the mares and their offspring, as far as they are eligible for the Stud Book, are entered. Breeders are bound to inform their Chairman, within three weeks, of any alteration in the number of horses kept by them, whether caused by sale, purchase, death or birth, on special forms supplied for this purpose; this, of course, applies only to those entered or eligible for entry

After a picture by Professor Volkers, Düsseldorf.

Flora, No. 1159, foaled 1889.
Sire: Wilko, No. 1101, Dam: Sylla, No. 1033.
Won 1892 I. State Prize also 4 prizes at the Shows at Bremen, Cologne and Berlin.
Sold to Estate Owner Böhmer, Wietzzyschowice, Russia.

in the Stud Book. The Chairman at once forwards this notice to the Secretary, so that it may be registered in the Stud Book.

The owners of registered mares are also obliged to communicate the date of foaling, on specially prepared cards, to the Chairman of their circuit, within six weeks; the Chairman then enters the foal in his register and sends the cards to the Secretary, who enters them in the Stud Book and gives a receipt for each foal. These receipts are then sent back to the Chairman; he and his colleagues appoint a time and place where the foals can be inspected to compare them as to sex, colour and markings, and if these tally with the Secretary's receipt the foals are branded on the near thigh with the mark of the Society, an O. with a simple crown above. Consequently all Oldenburg horses, entered or eligible for entry in the Stud Book, bear this mark.

Besides the Stud Book mark, there is another brand in use; namely for the stallions and mares that receive the State Premiums. This is an O. with a double divided crown and is placed on the off thigh. In addition to this, most of the Agricultural Societies in the district have their own brand, and when prizes are awarded at their Shows the horses and foals are usually marked on the near side of the neck.

After a picture by Professor Volkers, Düsseldorf.

Bildschön II., No. 9633, foaled 1897.
Sire: Andreas, No. 1317, Dam: Bildschön, No. 4210.
Won 1900 I. State Prize. International Show Paris 1900 II. Prize and Silver Medal.

The Regulations of 1897 introduced premiums for colt and filly foals, an innovation in the history of Oldenburg horse breeding; up to that date premiums had only been awarded to specially favoured stallions and mares, to keep them in the district. The sale of the best foals abroad had reached such dimensions that the breed was beginning to suffer in consequence, it was therefore found necessary to give premiums to foals to prevent, as far as possible, their being sold out of the country. The premiums for stallions and mares are paid out of the rates, those for foals are borne one half by the rates and the other by the Breeding Societies

3. For three and four year old mares, four first premiums value £ 25 each, five second premiums value £ 20 each and fourteen third premiums value £ 15 each.
4. For five to eight year old mares, six premiums value £ 15 each.
5. For two-year-old colts, four premiums of from £ 37.10.0 to £ 75.

Photograph by Feilner & Mohaupt, Oldenburg.

Gervin, No. 1557, foaled 1903.
Sire: Girello, No. 1414, Dam: Mete II., No. 8478.
Won Foal Prizes 1904 and 1905 and III. State Prize 1908.

The following premiums are given each year:

1. For four-year-old and over selected stallions,
   1st Prize £ 90 Preminum
   2nd „ £ 75 „
   3rd „ £ 60 „
2. For stallions which must be at least three years old and which have been selected for the first time first earnest or advance-money £ 37. 10. 0. second earnest money £ 30. 0. 0.
6. For yearling colts, six premiums value £ 20 each.
7. For yearling fillies, ten premiums value £ 7. 10. 0 each.
8. For colt-foals running with dam, eight premiums value £ 10 each.

Only specially suitable horses may be given premiums, the animals must be free from hereditary defects. The stallions which receive premiums must be kept for four, those to which earnest-money is given, two years, for service in the breeding district. Owners, who disobey this Regulation, have to return the premium and are also mulcted in a like sum as a fine to the Rates. The owner of a premium mare is also bound in like manner and must fulfil the following conditions, otherwise the fine is imposed.

1. He must agree to let the mare be served, for the next three years, by a premium stallion or by one chosen by the Selecting Committee.
2. The mare and her offspring, if the latter is still in the possession of the owner of the mare, must be brought before the Selecting Committee, for the same period as mentioned in paragraph 1, at the time appointed for the muster, the service-card for the current year has also to be shown.

The owner of a prize foal must also fulfil the following conditions, to avoid having to pay back the prize-money and being fined in a like amount.

1. For a colt-foal:
   a) The colt must not be sold to anyone outside the breeding district during the year it received the premium or the year following.
   b) To bring the colt to the annual Show and if it again gets a premium the owner is bound to accept it and also the conditions coupled with it.
   c) If it receives a premium when two to two-and-a-half years of age, it must be brought before the Selecting Committee when they hold their next muster, and if it is selected, it must then serve for a year in the district.
2. For filly-foals:
   a) They must not be sold outside the breeding district till they have reached maturity.
   b) They must be brought yearly to the fixtures appointed.
   c) They must be served when they are three years of age or soon after.

In the last few years premium-giving to colt-foals has been discontinued, owing to the fact the breeders in the district have been paying such high prices for them, that they have been kept in the country and there is no longer any fear that the best will be bought up to send abroad. The £ 80 that was formerly paid to the owners of colt-foals is now used to give extra prizes to yearling fillies.

To the before mentioned amounts given in premiums can be added £ 50 which is set aside to give three-year-old mares the opportunity of showing what they can do as trotters. The lowest record of these yearly trials hes been 1 km. (1092 yds) in three minutes, nearly all, where the animals have been well cared for, do better. It must be clearly understood that these trials do not in any way aspire to be trotting-matches, they are only intended to show purchasers that the Oldenburg horse, in spite of its weight and without being especially trained for the purpose is, in combination with high action, capable of covering the ground at a fair speed. There are several private societies, some of which have been in evidence for five years and over, which hold yearly Shows of their own and give prizes for trotting-competitions, thus incidentally bringing horse breeding to the fore.

It will be seen from the foregoing that the State and the breeders, helped by the laws and rates of the country, are working hand in hand to derive the highest possible result from an industry which contributes to the prosperity of the community at large.

6. Means of Communication, Disposal and Prices.

One of the chief factors, in the well-being of a country where horse and cattle-breeding is carried on to a large and successful extent, is that the means of communication between different parts are good and kept in repair. Not only has the State in Oldenburg recognised this from the beginning and acted accordingly, but also the District Councils work energetically in the same direction and spare neither time or money to gain the desired end. The whole country is covered with a network of excellent roads and railways, practically thought out so as to derive the greatest possible advantage from them. There is scarcely another part of Germany that can compare with

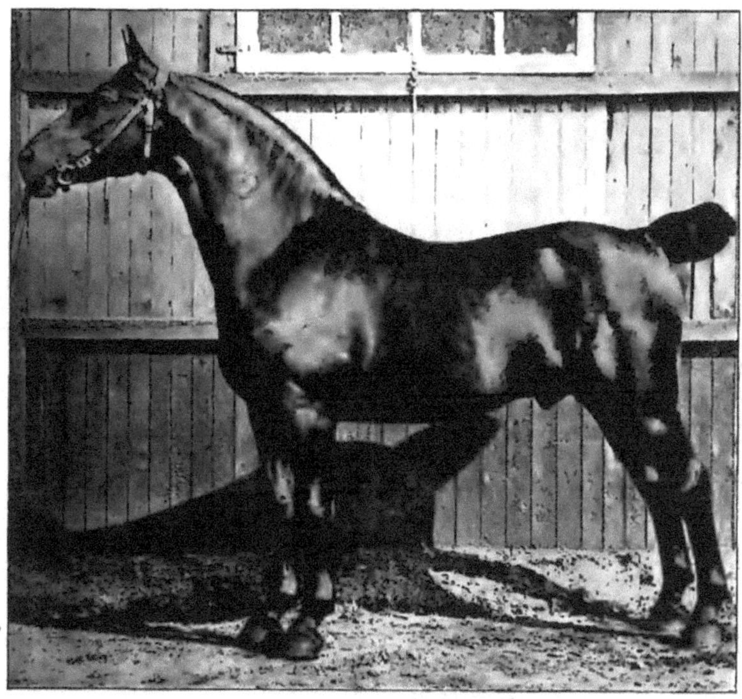

Photograph by J. Delton, Bois de Boulogne.

Botho, No. 1354, foaled 1894.
Sire: Bravo, No. 1481, Dam: Gradiska, 3691.
Won 1897 I. Advance-Money Premium, 1899 II. State Prize and at the International Show at Paris 1900 I. Prize and Gold Medal.
Botho was sold to go to Holland in 1903.

Oldenburg in this respect. A glance at the map of the breeding district, at the end of the book, will convince the reader that this assertion is correct. Flourishing villages, often nearly as large as small towns, which possess clean, well-kept hotels for the benefit of travellers, are to be found conveniently situated in almost every part of the country. On this account, it is easy for intending purchasers to travel in the breeding district, even at the worst time in the year, and see the stock at grass or in the breeders' stables and choose for themselves. It is also possible for the breeders to take their stock in good condition to the various markets to show or dispose of them there, without much trouble as would be the case if the roads were bad.

The chief horse-fairs in the districts are held at Jever, Oldenburg, Ovelgönne and Varel. Older horses are to be had at all these, whereas the principal fair for yearling colts is the so-called Medardus Market held at Oldenburg at the commencement of June each year: for eighteen months old fillies and foals of the year the autumn fairs held at Oldenburg, Ovelgönne and Varel are considered the best. Particular attention, however, in drawn to the fact that

Photograph by Fellner & Mohaupt, Oldenburg.

Edelmann, No. 1527, foaled 1901.
Sire: Ehrenberg, No. 1383, Dam: Schlange, No. 1065.
Won 1904 II. Advance-Money Premium and 1907 III. State Prize.

at these last mentioned markets, most of the horses in the eighteen months old class are already in the possession of horse-dealers who have bought up the animals and take them off the hands of the breeders a few days before the fair at places appointed for that purpose. These so-called "early markets" are gaining in importance from year to year, to the detriment of the real fixtures; it cannot, therefore, be too strongly impressed on intending purchasers that they should visit these "early markets", so as to see the best that is to be had.

Another good opportunity of buying two-year-old and younger animals is at the local Shows, usually held at the end of the summer. We only mention those of Stollhamm, Ovelgönne, Berne, Oldenburg and Jever as being the largest and best known of the many that take place.

Each year, at the end of January or beginning of February, the State Selecting Committee has the stallions brought to Oldenburg for selection. In course of time this has become a recognised opportunity for the sale of the same; on an average about 300 stallions are brought together, amongst which some 250 three-year-olds which, as yet, have not been selected. Buyers for foreign Studs often purchase their rising three-year-olds in early summer or a little later in the year, in the first place because there are then more animals to choose from and secondly, the horses have more time to get accustomed to their new surroundings before being used for breeding purposes the next spring. This also applies to the American importers, especially as they can make their purchases in France and Belgium about the same time.

If foreign buyers, particularly those sent to buy up horses for a foreign Government, wish to see and buy a large number of horses without going to Shows or Horse

Photograph by Fellner & Mohaupt, Oldenburg.

Stallion Fair at Rodenkirchen at the time of the visit of the Croatian-Slavonian Purchase Commissioners for the Royal Stud at Agram in the year 1909.

Fairs for that purpose, the Council of the Stud Book is usually prepared to make arrangements with the breeders to bring their animals to a place where they can be conveniently seen and compared and to issue private catalogues to make the selection of unrelated horses easier.

The prices for Oldenburgs vary considerably; it is, therefore, almost impossible to give an average figure. Pedigree plays a very important part in determining the price, more especially for those kept in the district for breeding purposes. Amounts of £ 1500, £ 1250, £ 1000, £ 900 — in this year even £ 1625 — have been paid, not only by a Breeder's Society but also by private persons. £ 150 is sometimes paid for a two to three-year-old fillies and £ 60 to £ 100 for filly foals, these prices are, however, unusual. With such prices ruling in the district it is not much wonder that foreigners do not care to compete for the very best animals. If we exclude such exceptional animals, the prices paid for three-year-olds, for service in the district, vary from £ 200 to £ 400; as, however, only about a dozen such are required each year, there is a large number of excellent three-year-old stallions to be had ranging from £ 200 downwards. A good percentage are sold to go abroad when they are two-year-olds; these fetch on an average about £ 100, but sometimes as much as £ 200 is obtained for them. The present price for 18 months old colts is from £ 40 to £ 50, good colt-foals, 4—7 months of age, are to be had from £ 25 to £ 40. Good three-year-old and older geldings fetch from £ 50 upwards. Mares of three years and upwards change hands at from £ 60 to £ 90, two-year-old fillies from £ 50 to £ 60; it is not often, however, that this class of animal is offered for sale. The generality of 18 months old fillies bring £ 25 to £ 37.10.0, filly foals 4—7 months of age from £ 15 to £ 25.

7. The Oldenburg Horse in the Neighbouring Breeding Districts of Bremen and East Friesland, in the Army and Abroad.

Considering the great esteem in which the Oldenburg horse has always been held, it is small wonder that its influence has been extended

Photograph by Feilner & Mohaupt, Oldenburg.

Kuno, No. 1537, foaled 1902.
Sire: Kurfürst, No. 1443, Dam: Tasmana II., No. 7927.
Won 1904 Foal Premium, 1905 II. Advance-Money Premium, at the Shows of the German Agricultural Society Munich 1905 and Strassburg 1913 I. Prize and in 1907 III. State Prize.

to the neighbouring provinces across our borders. The farmers in Bremen and East Friesland have much the same soil and climatic conditions to work on as we have, and for this reason, when buying breeding material, give the preference to Oldenburg horses. There are many purebred Oldenburgs in the Bremen district, their owners having even placed themselves under the Oldenburg Regulations in respect to horse breeding, so as to enjoy the benefits of being members of the Stud Book Society. In such a small area as Bremen possesses, however, it is evident that horse breeding cannot play such an important part as it

Photograph by G. Backhaus, Jade.

Three-year-old Colt **Erasmus**, No. 1871, foaled 1906.
Sire: Elimar, No. 1541, Dam: Gehülfin II., No. 9724. Won Foal Premium 1904.

Photograph by G. Backhaus Jade.

Elimar, No. 1541, foaled 1902.
Sire: Elegant, No. 1387, Dam: Orsina, No. 7206.
Won 1903/4 Foal Premiums, 1905 I. Advance-Money Premium and 1907 II. State Prize.

does amongst our western neighbours in East Friesland.

The East Frisian horse is very like the Oldenburg; it has almost the same blood in its veins. For this reason it can be easily understood that a great number of horses that were bred in Oldenburg, but reared in East Friesland, are chosen yearly by the East Frisian Selecting Committee to serve in their country and are often kept for further use by the payment of high retaining-premiums. It is the same with the pure-bred Oldenburg broodmares, they are kept in the country by money payments. As the East Frisian Stud Book, (Vols. II. and III. from 1897 to 1908) shows, that of the 315 stallions selected by the East Frisian Selecting Committee, no less than 168, of which 34 had received premiums. were pure Oldenburgs, which is a clear proof of the influence the Oldenburg exercises to this day in East Frisian horse breeding. A further proof in this direction can be learnt from the book on the East Frisian Horse issued in 1907, which gives, besides pictures of the various crosses between East Frisian and Oldenburg horses, also those of pure-bred Oldenburgs. (Page 24: "Morra II." page 40: "Rheiderland" and page 102: "Lambert".)

Photograph by Feilner & Mohaupt, Oldenburg.

Gilbert, No. 1405, foaled 1897.
Sire: Wittelsbacher, No. 1525, Dam: Rama, No. 7925.

But it is not alone in the countries bordering on Oldenburg that its horse is valued. Every year numbers of connoisseurs come from nearly every State in Germany, where horse breeding is carried on, as also from various parts of the world, to buy fresh blood. For instance, as we are informed by the Ministry of Agriculture for the Kingdom of Prussia, that during the last 20 years, 740 Oldenburg stallions have been bought for use in the Royal Stud Farms.

From statistics supplied to us by the Manager of the Royal Stud Farms in Bavaria in September 1907, it appears that since 1874 no less than 682 Oldenburg stallions have been bought for use in that country. The letter goes on to say:

"It must be allowed that these Oldenburg sires transferred their good qualities to their offspring in general; in particular, the free and powerful action, as well as the weight of their progeny, has given great satisfaction. The importation of these horses has helped to bring horse breeding into favour, more especially in the Government Department of Lower Bavaria and also in a part of Upper Bavaria. Their form, strength of bone and free action are highly prized; for this reason higher prices are often given for them than the military authorities can at present pay for Army horses."

Photograph by Feilner & Mohaupt, Oldenburg.

Asco, No. 1357, foaled 1895.
Sire: Coco, No. 1274, Dam: Waisenkind, No. 2183.
Won 1898 II. Advance-Money Premium and 1900 III. State Prize.
Asco was sold to the Royal Stud at Moritzburg, Saxony, in 1903.

Since 1907 a large number of Oldenburg horses have been bought yearly for the Bavarian Studs.

The estimation in which the Oldenburg in the Kingdom of Saxony is held, where a great many stallions, as well as 18 months old fillies and older mares, have been imported during a number of years, is shown by the following official document, written in 1907 by the Director of the Royal Studs of Saxony and addressed to the Grand Ducal Ministry at Oldenburg:

"The inquiry of the Grand Ducal Ministry of the 16th September 1907, on behalf of the Oldenburg

Photograph by F. A. Schwartz, Berlin.

Oldenburg Remount (Artillery Shaft-Horse).
Sire: Ailrat, No. 1193.

Stud Book Society,*) has been duly received and we are instructed to inform you that the first Oldenburg stallions were imported into Saxony in 1871. Since that date, a number of stallions have been bought each year in Oldenburg, so that a total of 256 in all have been imported and used for Stud purposes in the Kingdom of Saxony.

Regarding the influence these animals have had on horse breeding in our country and why it was that Oldenburgs were chosen to improve the quality of the very mixed material we had in our mares. was

1. that the stallion must be capable of improving not only the progeny of one class of mare but of many kinds,
2. that the offspring must be animals that could be used for farm work,
3. that the females sired by these stallions, must in their turn be capable of producing not only animals that were to be of use on the farm, but also

*) Concerning the number of horses bought and the influence produced by them at the Moritzburg Stud.

of giving birth to horses that could afterwards be bought as remounts, more especially for the Artillery,

4. that in districts in which the breeding of heavy cart horses was not a speciality, breeding from cart horse stallions might be discontinued, in the favour of Oldenburgs."

As regards Nos. 1 and 2 we may remark that the Oldenburgs have done all that was expected of them and that the results have justified their importation; but this improvement has only taken place where rather short legged, correctly built, showy horses have been used, the ones of heavier build and of less good appearance, have not been a success.

It is also indisputable that the Oldenburg is a good foundation for the production of brood mares. It has been proved beyond doubt that his progeny are much more useful for breeding purposes later on, than is that of a heavy Hanover stallion.

The Oldenburg has, however, proved to be most useful where it was the object to oust the cart horse and to prevent his crossing with unsuitable material. It is certain that no other horse but the Oldenburg, could have accomplished this and induced the breeders to refrain from breeding cart horses in Saxony: in most parts of this kingdom a cart horse, pure and simple, is not needed for the work it is required to perform.

After a picture by Professor Volkers, Düsseldorf.

Anziehung, No. 4406, foaled 1892.
Sire: Admiral, No. 1110, Dam: Arsena, No. 1084.
Won two I. State Prizes. Paris International Show 1900,
IV. Prize and Bronze Medal.

The question as to the quality of the Oldenburg for remount requirements can be answered as follows: The Remount Department of Saxony, as a body, do not care to buy horses with Oldenburg blood in their veins, because they hold the view that this horse has not quite enough breeding in most cases for their purpose. This is not to be wondered at, because in many instances the mares they are used on are not nearly so well bred as they are. In spite of this, the influence of the Oldenburg on remounts is much greater than most people imagine, because he is often the agent in producing really useful material from ordinary mares and thus laying the foundation on which nobler blood can be used to greater advantage. As a matter of fact, the influence of the Oldenburg, in this respect, is a particularly good one; we take for example the result of the prizes given to the remounts bought this year, as follows:

"Of the 48 mares bought in this year by the Remount Department 19 were born in Saxony and were the progeny of stallions bought by the Royal Stud.

Of these 19 mares

17 are the descendants of Oldenburg stallions,

1 from a Holstein stallion and

1 from a Normandy stallion.

Thus, from 16 Remounts that received prizes, 9 were the offspring of mares that were sired by Oldenburgs, and from 9 that won 1st prizes, 7 were of the same origin."

The Remount Department buys horses each year in our district and this shows that the Oldenburgs are becoming much more sought after for Army purposes. The Prussian War Office was asked by the Council of the Stud Book Society to allow their Remount Department to give their experience as to the use of Oldenburg horses. The following answer was sent to the Grand Ducal Ministry at Oldenburg:

"The Remounts and older horses, bought in the last ten years in Oldenburg, have shown a great improvement in the way they have been bred; they are decidedly more noble in character and this has been accomplished without loss of weight, the action is better, flat hoofs and knees are less frequent. The Oldenburg Remounts etc. are used only for the Field Artillery and are good service horses. They have smooth action, are easily trained, are useful draught horses, throwing plenty of weight into their work and are good "doers".

Amongst European purchasers Holland may be mentioned as a very good customer. Italy, Austria, Switzerland, Russia, Denmark and Sweden also take our horses, in some cases even they breed them quite pure. In the six volumes of the "Paardenstambock" (Stud Book) published since 1897, of the Dutch province of Groningen, of 147 stallions entered, 90 are either pure bred Oldenburgs or of Oldenburg extraction, and in the sixth volume of 402 mares entered 307 have Oldenburg blood on their side.

Our coach horses are also to be met with in England. The well-known English breeder, Sir Walter Gilbey, who bought two three-year-old Oldenburg fillies, one of which "Erra II." won the Champion Prize, at the International Exhibition at Paris, for £ 500, says in his book, "Horse Breeding in England and India and Army Horses Abroad":

"Hundreds of pairs of carriage and coach horses have been sold every year in London at from £ 200 to £ 500 a pair, the purchasers being quite unaware of their foreign origin. At recent sales brown and bay upstanding coach horses from coaches running during the summer out of London have sold at from 100 to 200 guineas; a pair purchased by a friend cost 350 guineas. There can be no doubt whatever where these animals were bred; if anyone took the trouble to trace their pedigree it would be found that they came either from the Oldenburg province of Germany, or from the horse breeding districts of Normandy in France; there can be no mistaking the breeds.".

Joh. Böning, Neuenbrok, 88 years of age, the oldest and most worthy Oldenburg stallion keeper.

Rotbart, No. 1456, foaled 1899. *Photograph by Feilner & Mohaupt, Oldenburg.*
Sire: Ruthard, No. 1155, Dam: Johila, No. 4937. III. State Prize.
Sold to the Royal Stud at Moritzburg, Saxony, in 1906.

In Austria our horses have been well known for many years: at the International Stallion Show at Vienna they found ready buyers. In latter times, the Austrian Board of Agriculture has bought up numbers of stallions in Oldenburg. A new market has lately been found for our horses in the Austrian Kingdom of Croatia. For the past few years the Government has sent a deputation of officers to buy horses for the Royal Stud Depot at Agram. The carefully selected animals have given great satisfaction in Croatia; the offspring of these stallions has turned out to be of excellent quality and there is every sign that this country will be a good customer in the future.

Across the seas, the Oldenburg has been in great demand during the last ten years. It was Lübben, Sürwürden who first exported Oldenburgs; he was also the first exhibitor of these horses at various Shows in North and South America, Australia and even in Africa, his animals won the highest honours; by sending to these various countries. Lübben was the pioneer who opened the world's markets to the Oldenburg horse. The agents of well-known foreign firms come each year to buy horses in our district. Since 1888 about 2000 Oldenburgs, mostly stallions, have been exported to America; the result has been most satisfactory. whether they have been kept pure or crossed with other breeds; especially when crossed with trotters their progeny has been most successful in winning the highest prizes at Shows. Taking all these considerations into account there seems a fair prospect that this market will be kept open for the Oldenburg horse; of course it will be liable to fluctuations dependent on the laws of supply and demand in America.

8. Promotion of Horse Breeding under the Dukes of Oldenburg.

All Oldenburg Princes have been interested in the development of horse breeding in the country since the Middle Ages. The present ruler, the Grand Duke Friedrich August, is a great connoisseur of horses and does everything he can to promote the improvement of the breed. On the big occasions, when the best of the horses are brought together to be selected each year in Oldenburg and where thousands of breeders meet, the Grand Duke is always amongst them, and after the judging is over has all the prize- winners led past him: he examines each animal carefully. The Grand Duke also does his best to keep promising young colts in the country; in the year 1901 he started a rearing establishment for 18 months old colts on his estate at "Bungsberghof". Each year twelve of the best animals obtainable are bought for him and kept at his farm till they are three years of age; he then enters them for selection and they have to compete against the best material in the country passing under the critical observation of the Selecting Committee in common with others. The private "Society for the Improvement of the Oldenburg Horse", which has now been for many years in existence, stands under the protection of the Grand Duke. This Society holds its own Riding, Driving and Jumping Competition each year; the Grand Duke is a regular attendant at these meetings.

Photograph by Feilner & Mohaupt, Oldenburg.

Three-year-old Oldenburg Filly **Atalante,** No. 15746.
Sire: Freiherr, No. 1511; Dam: Adelphine III., No. 12733.
Won III. State Prize in 1909.

9. Results at Shows and Honours Conferred.

Large Gold Medal.

Small Gold Medal.

Won by Oldenburg Horses at the International Show at Paris.

Wherever the Oldenburg horse has been exhibited either at home or abroad, he has always met with astonishing success. It is not only that individual horses gained honours, but that the collection, as a whole, has been of such equality as to command attention and surprise. The uniformity of any breed however, is the best possible criterion as to its value. Later on, we give a list of the prizes won at various Shows by the Oldenburgs. In the meantime we will confine ourselves to the Reports of the German Agricultural Society issued in their Yearly Journal, because in these the uniformity of the Oldenburg horse has always been particularly noticed.

In he report of Count Bismarck, Ihringen (Baden) concerning horses at the Show of the German Agricultural Society held at Frankfurt in 1899, he says, "The Holstein Marsh Horse Breeders' Society were as usual to the fore and exhibited some very fine animals, which on account of their good action were well thought of; at the same time, however, their uniformity of type could not nearly come up to that of the Oldenburgs".

In the report of Count Bismarck. at Halle a. S. Privy-Counsellor Dr. Lydtin, Baden-Baden, writes. amongst other things, "Quite another picture met our gaze as we turned to Class 9, set aside for three-year-old fillies of the carriage horse type. In this class, the six whole browns and one black filly*) completely overshadowed the rest, *they all appeared to have been cast in one mould*".

Of the Show in Hanover in 1903 the Chief Master of the Horse von Wenckstern, Oldenburg, says in his report, "As has always been the case up to the present, the horses belonging to the Oldenburg Horse Breeders' Society have taken the first place in the classes where they can be exhibited. *They are a wonderfully even lot*, this was especially noticeable in the two-year-old class. The early maturity of this breed was shown to special advantage here, no other could touch them in this respect."

Herr Rittergutsbesitzer Hillmann, Nordenthal, (East Prussia), issued the following Report concerning the collection of Oldenburg horses at the Show held at Munich in 1905, stating that the only two breeds that competed for the Collection Prize were those of the Holstein Marsh and Oldenburg Breeders' Societies: "Both Collections showed *great uniformity of type*, and were nearly equal in quality, the Oldenburgs were however able to secure the first prize, owing to their size and also to the fact that they gained more honours in the single classes". It was at the Show at Düsseldorf in 1907, that the Oldenburg horses had the hardest battle to fight for the Collection Prize; the well-known Hippologe Professor Dr. von Nathusius, Jena, reports, amongst other things, as follows: —

"Three two-year-old, four three-year-old fillies and two two-year-old colts were shown at Düsseldorf to compete for the Collection Prize, Their *uniformity was quite perfect*; to show, however, that we were not deceived by outward appearance, colour, etc., etc., I should like to point out the most extraordinary evenness of their weights, they were weighed in the Show Yard. The three-year-old fillies scaled:

cwt.	qr.	lb.
11	2	1
11	2	1
11	2	12
11	3	24

*) Sent by the Oldenburg Horse Breeders' Society.

A. Front.

B. Reverse.

The medal awarded to the Oldenburg Horse-Breeders' Association at the World's Fair St. Louis 1904.

the two-year-old fillies:

cwt.	qr.	lb.
11	0	0
11	0	11
11	0	22

One of the colts scaled:

cwt.	qr.	lb.
11	2	20

the other was not weighed; in fact I cannot remember having seen him. I do not mind being thought singular for laying stress on the weights of these horses; on the contrary, I take it as a convincing proof, that the striking uniformity that was visible to the naked eye, has been confirmed beyond doubt by the surer method of the scales.

It was a particular satisfaction to me to find that my judgment of these animals was correct. In the report I made to the Horse Committee at the Show, I said, the Oldenburgs are more compact and better bred than I have ever noticed before. As I write this, I have the reports of the Shows at Hanover and Halle before me and I find that the weights and measurements of the animals shown there were much heavier and larger than those shown at Düsseldorf; this was especially noticeable in the breadth of chest and shank or cannon-bone

Diploma won by the Oldenburg Horse Breeders' Society at the International Show at St. Louis, 1904.

circumference. As the climate and nature of the soil in Oldenburg prevents their horses becoming too fine in body and limb, the breeders need not fear that their coach horse is deteriorating, when now and then a more elegant animal is bred. The Stallion, Catalogue No. 70, was perhaps too light for the service required of him. The mares were quite heavy enough. three of the three-year-old fillies were able to beat their East Frisian opponents and take the first prize; also in the two-year-old class No. 20, the catalogue number 73 won the first prize, no other prizes were available.

That the Oldenburgs were bound to carry off the first Collection Prize was clear; even if so many really good animals hat not been to the fore, their uniformity alone would have turned the balance in their favour. It is worthy of remark that the two first prize mares were sired by the same Stallion "Erbgraf No. 1500". It is not necessary to go into details further than to say that their good fore-legs and regular action deserve the highest praise.

I made the remark at the beginning of my report that it was not desirable to enter too many animals for the Collection Prize, this has been fully justified by the success of the Oldenburgs with their small selection of nine animals only."

In like manner, this same gentleman makes his report about horses at the Show of the German Agricultural Society held at Leipzig in 1909. Here, the Oldenburg horses bred in Saxony, competed for the first time at a Show of the German Agricultural Society and with great success. Horse breeding had been carried on for decades in Saxony, with Oldenburg blood as a foundation, it is therefore appropriate to quote the success attained by this breed.

Thirty-six horses were exhibited by the Foal Rearing Society for the Kingdom of Saxony from their farm at Moritzburg, they won: 6 Champion Prizes, 1st Collection Prize, 3 first, 6 second, 1 third and 1 fourth prizes besides being 5 times highly commended.

The following passage is quoted from the Report of the competent judge at this Show:

"Horse breeding in the Kingdom of Saxony, as you all know, has been built up during the last few decades by the use of Oldenburg blood. That horse breeding is difficult in Saxony, owing to the conditions of both soil and climate, is acknowledged; it is therefore all the more creditable that such good results have been obtained. If one looks at the Collections as they are being paraded, one does not feel one's self looking at a uniform collection of Oldenburg horses. I, at least, for my part, never seemed to be doing so. It is otherwise when one looks at the animals individually, as a great many of them are of a practical and useful type, while others are stylish and handsome. It was an eye-opener to me that such really fine saddle horses, as a great many of them are, could be descended from the Oldenburgs. I am not saying this in disparagement of the Oldenburgs; on the contrary, I mean it to be taken as praise: as it is a well known fact that saddle horses are, of all others, the most difficult to breed."

We cannot conclude the chapter better than by mentioning a memorable circumstance in the history of the Oldenburg horse.

At the time when the whole German race thronged to do honour to Prince Bismarck on his 80th birthday and to shower congratulations and gifts upon him, the Oldenburg horse was also called upon to play its part. On the 27th April 1895 Prince Bismarck received 1820 representatives of the Duchy of Oldenburg who presented him with two choice mares with foals at foot. The Prince was much touched at this token of love and appreciation as well as by the illuminated address which was handed to him at the same time: it read as follows:

"From the faithful Oldenburgers to his Serene Highness Prince Otto von Bismarck on his 80th birthday.

Most Serene Highness and Prince!

On this auspicious day of rejoicing, at a time when the united peoples and races of Germany approach, with thankful hearts, to offer your Serene Highness their sincere congratulations and to show their appreciation of their greatest Statesman on his 80th birthday, so we also wish to give expression to our feelings of thanks and veneration. The land which forms our Home is small indeed but stedfast in patriotism to the German Fatherland and happy in the consciousness of belonging to so mighty an Empire. We are proud of the fact of living in Oldenburg as subjects of a far-seeing Ruler. At the same time, however, we consider it an inestimable advantage to share in the strong protection and blessings afforded us as the result of German Unity. This has principally been accomplished by the wise councils and untiring efforts of Your Serene Highness. We therefore respectfully approach Your Serene Highness to beg the acceptance of a practical expression of our gratitude. The noblest product of our native land for centuries has been the Horse, the pride and joy of our Agriculture. This seemed the most appropriate gift to offer to the most noble citizen of the German Empire and to the Prince who is himself a farmer. May the choice mares selected by us and their progeny long give pleasure to your Serene Highness and also afford a proof of the unalterable fidelity that the people of the Grand Duchy of Oldenburg entertain for Prince Bismarck. From this country also the prayer ascends to Heaven,

God bless and save Your
Serene Highness."

As during the Thirty Years' War Count Anton Günther presented his noblest horses to the German Emperor, the King of Sweden and their generals to emphasize his wishes but more especially to keep both the Emperor's and King's armies from invading his country, so in like manner, after a lapse of 300 years, the people of Oldenburg thought that their Noble Horse "was the most fitting gift to the Founder of the German Empire". Truly a significant sign of the importance and regard in which the Horse is held in Oldenburg.

List of Honours.

At Shows, outside their own country, Oldenburg horses have won, amongst others, the following prizes:

International Show at Hamburg 1863. 1 II., 3 H.C's.

International Show at Bremen 1874. 7 I., 10 II., 8 III., 4 IV., 1 Special Prize.

International Show at Hamburg 1883. 1 I., 3 II., 2 III.

International Show at Amsterdam 1884. 2 I., 1 II., 1 III., 3 Silver Medals and Collection Prize.

International Show at Buenos Aires 1886. 3 I.

Migratory Show of the German Agricultural Society Frankfurt a. M.

1887. 4 I., 3 II., 2 III., 3 H.C's, 1 Special, 1 Collection Prize.

Chicago Show 1888. 1 I.

Universal German Horse Show Berlin 1890. 3 I., 2 II., 4 III., 3 IV., 2 Special Prizes.

International Show at Buenos Aires 1890. 3 I.

Migratory Show of the German Agricultural Society, Bremen 1893. 8 I., 5 II., 5 III., 6 H.C's and a Special Prize.

Migratory Show of the German Agricultural Society, Munich 1893. 1 I., 1 II., 1 III., 1 IV., 2 H.C's, 1st Collection Prize.

International Show Chicago 1893. 4 I., 3 II., 3 III., 3 V., 2 Champion, 1st Collection Prize, 1 II. Special Prize.

Migratory Show of the German Agricultural Society, Berlin 1894. 1 I., 2 II., 1 III., H.C., 2nd Collection Prize, 1 Champion Prize.

Migratory Show of the German Agricultural Society, Cologne a. R. 1895. 2 I., 5 II., 1 III., 1 IV., 1 Extra Prize and Gold Medal.

Moscow Show 1895. Gold Medal.

Migratory Show of the German Agricultural Society, Stuttgart 1896. 1 I., 2 II., 2 III., 1 IV., 1st Collection, 1 Champion, 1 Special Prize.

Port Elizabeth (South Africa) Show 1896. 1 I.

Migratory Show of the German Agricultural Society, Hamburg 1897. 3 I., 4 II., 3 III., 2 IV., 2 Collection, 1 Champion and 1 Extra Prize.

Sidney (Australia) Show 1897. 1 I.

Buenos Aires Show 1898. 3 I.

Migratory Show of the German Agricultural Society, Dresden 1898. 2 I. (one of which was a Family Prize), 1 II., 2 III., 1 H.C.

Migratory Show of the German Agricultural Society, Frankfurt a. M. 1899. 1 I., 4 II., 4 III., 1 IV., 4 H.C's, 1st Collection Prize.

International Show Paris 1900. 1 I., 2 II., 1 III., 1 IV., 4 Diplomas, 4 Gold Medals, 1 Silver Medal, 1 Bronze Medal, and the Champion Prize for half-bred mares.

Migratory Show of the German Agricultural Society Halle a. S. 1901. 5 I., 2 II., 2 III., 1st Collection and 1 Champion Prize.

Rostow a. Don. Show 1901. Gold Medal.

Migratory Show of the German Agricultural Society, Hanover 1903. 5 I., 4 II., 1 III., 2 IV., 7 H.C's, 2 1st Family Prizes, II. Collection Prize.

Charkow (South Russia) Show. 2 gold and 2 silver medals.

International Show St. Louis 1904. 7 I., 5 II., 3 III., 1 IV., 2 Specials, 3 1st Champion, 3 II. Champion, 1 1st Grand Champion, 2 II. Grand Champion, 1st Championship Honors (for the best show of German coach horses).

The Oldenburg Stallion "Hannibal" (Sire: Andreas, Dam: Leontine No. 3481) shown by Mr. Crouch, La Fafyette, won a first Grand Champion Prize.

Rostow and Moscow Shows 1904. 2 gold and 2 silver medals.

Migratory Show of the German Agricultural Society, Munich 1905. 4 I., 3 II., 1 III., 1 IV., 2 H.C's, 1 Champion and 2 1st Collection Prizes.

Migratory Show of the German Agricultural Society, Berlin 1906. 5 I., 6 II., 1 III., 6 H.C's, 1 1st Collection, 1 I. Champion.

Migratory Show of the German Agricultural Society, Düsseldorf 1907. 2 I., 1 II., 1 III., 1 H.C., 1 I. Collection and Extra Prize for the best Collection.

Migratory Show of the German Agricultural Society, Stuttgart 1908. 2 I., 2 H.C's, 1 I. Collection.

Migratory Show of the German Agricultural Society, Leipzig 1909. 1 I., 2 II., 2 H.C's, 1 I. Collection and Special Prize.

Rostow and Poltawa Shows 1909. 2 gold medals.

International Show Buenos Aires 1910. 2 I., 1 II., 1 III. and Champion Prize.

Migratory Show of the German Agricultural Society Hamburg 1910. 5 I., 5 II., 2 III., 5 IV., 3 Champion, 2 I. Collection Prizes, 3 Family Prizes.

Migratory Show of the German Agricultural Society Cassel 1911. 4 I., 2 II., 1 IV., 1 Champion, 1 I. Collection Prize, 1 Extra Prize.

Migratory Show of the German Agricultural Society Strassburg 1913. 5 I., 1 II., 2 IV., 1 Champion, 2 I. Collection Prizes.

Covered thus with honours, the Oldenburg horse has become known throughout the civilised world; its breeders are determined to follow the example set them by their forefathers to keep their horses true to the old type which has been so successful for generations; they think they are justified in casting the following horoscope: As the Oldenburg is the strongest and most consistently bred of all German coach horses, it appears to be destined and fitted to restore all other breeds that have in the course of time lost strength of bone and weight.

Photograph by Feilner & Mohaupt, Oldenburg.

Three-year-old Colt **Erbprinz**, No. 1874, foaled 1906.
Sire: Erbgraf, No. 1500, Dam: Pyrola III., No. 10265.
Won 1906, 1907, 1908 Foal Premiums, 1909 I. Advance-Money Premium and 1911 I. State Prize.

10. Regulations Concerning Horse Breeding in Oldenburg.

I. General Rules.

Paragraph 1.

The improvement of horse breeding is to be accomplished in the following ways:

A) Selection of stallions and regulating use of same.
B) Giving Premiums for really good stallions and mares and for breeding suitable foals.
C) Prizes for Competitions.
D) Entering suitable horses in the Stud Book.
E) Subsidies to help breeders to buy stallions, fillies and filly foals.

Paragraph 2.

The Duchy of Oldenburg to be divided into two breeding districts, the North and the South. The boundaries to be suggested by the Selecting Committee and to be made absolute by the Ministry of State, Home Department.

Paragraph 3.

The Selecting Committee stands under the direct control of the Ministry of State, Home Department; it is answerable for the selection of Stallions as well as settling which stallions and mares are to receive the premiums, also to carry into effect all rules for the improvement of horse breeding as mentioned in Paragraph 1.

The Selecting Committee is also the approved medium for making representations to the Government for the improvement of horse breeding and is at the same time bound to give its opinion on the subject under consideration.

Paragraph 4.

§ 1. The Selecting Committee is composed of three permanent members and three elected or chosen members each for the northern and southern districts, these last are changed from time to time, each elected member has a proxy in case he cannot attend on all occasions.

§ 2. The permanent members are appointed by the Ministry of State, one of whom is the Chairman. If one of these members is absent, the Chairman has the option of selecting a non-permanent member to take his place for the time being.

§ 3. For each of the two breeding districts the Council of the Stud Book Society in each case has the privilege of nominating nine persons, who possess a thorough knowledge of horses, to act on the Selecting Committee as non-permanent members; from these nine the Ministry of State, Home Department, select three as members and three as proxies for each division. No person who gets his living principally by the sale of horses (in other words, a horse dealer), though he may be a breeder as well, is allowed to be nominated for this office. As far as is conveniently possible, care is taken that each part of the district is fairly represented on the Selecting Committee.

§ 4. The non-permanent members and their proxies serve for a period of six years. In case a member cannot act, his proxy has to take his place; this also holds good when a non-permanent member (§ 2) has to take the place of a permanent one. If, through any cause, a non-permanent member is prevented from serving fo the whole period of his six years, his proxy takes his place; the Ministry of State, Home Department, then decides if it is necessary to choose another proxy to fill the vacancy. (§ 3.)

§ 5. The duty of serving on the Selcting Committee by non-permanent members and their proxies is compulsory, unless:

1. they have served for a period of six years, as non-permanent members, immediately preceding the new appointment to office,
2. they are 65 years of age,
3. they can show just cause why they should not serve, they have to satisfy the Ministry of State, Home Department, on this point however. Anyone who refuses to act or lays down his office during the time of his service can be fined a sum not exceeding **£** 7. 10. 0, the Ministry of State. Home Department, determines the amount of the fine.

§ 6. The permanent members of the Selecting Committee as well as the Veterinary Inspectors (Paragraph 6, Paragraph 11, § 4) employed to examine the horses, if they are not already in the service of the State, have to make an affirmation before the Ministry of State, Home Department, that they will carry out their duties conscientiously and faithfully, the non-permanent members and their proxies do the same before the magistrates of their respective districts.

Paragraph 5.

§ 1. The Selecting Committee pass their resolutions by voting; if the votes are equal, the Chairman has the casting one.

§ 2. All decisions of the Selecting Committee are taken down in writing, a clerk is lent for this purpose by the Ministry of State, Home Department.

§ 3. The Selecting Committee has the right to determine time and place where the horses are to be brought together for inspection and can impose a fine of **£ 1** on anyone who does not bring his horse or horses to the parade, adequate notice of these meetings has to be given.

§ 4. The Selecting Committee receive their instructions through the Ministry of State, Home Department.

Paragraph 6.

Before the Selecting parade takes place, all the horses ordered to attend, have to be examined by the Veterinary Inspector, appointed by the Ministry of State, Home Department, as to their health and fitness.

The veterinary examination is held at a time and place suggested by the Selecting Committee and approved of by the Ministry of State, Home Department.

Paragraph 7.

The members of the Selecting Committee and Veterinary Inspectors (Paragraphs 6 and 11, § 4) receive travelling expenses and a fixed sum daily, the amount of which is determined by the Ministry of State, Home Department.

II. Special Resolutions.

A. Selection of Stallions and Manner in which they are to be Used. Regular Selection and Secondary Selection.

Paragraph 8.

§ 1. The only Stallions allowed to be used for breeding purposes are those that have been approved (chosen) by the Selecting Committee and passed as sound.

§ 2. An exception to § 1 can be made if a breeder keeps a stallion for his own use only.

If however a non-selected stallion or a stallion that has been selected, but cast by the Selecting Committee, is the joint property of several breeders, he can only be used by the person on whose farm he stands and for his mares only; he may not be removed to another farm during the Season without the consent of the Selecting Committee.

§ 3. Only such stallions may be presented for selection which satisfy the demands made by the Ministry of State, Home Department. Foreign horses are eligible for selection if the Selecting Committee consider they are likely to improve the home breed.

§ 4. The Selecting Committee has the right of having the progeny of a selected stallion paraded before them.

§ 5. If a stallion has not been selected he may not be brought before the Committee a second time, this does not apply to three-year-old colts, these may be sent again. With the permission of the Ministry of State, Home Department, older horses, that have once been selected but suspended from service for a time, can again be chosen for service if it can be proved that their offspring has been of value to the breed in the district.

Paragraph 9.

§ 1. The regular selecting parade is held during the first three months of each year, at a place or places determined by the Selecting Committee.

§ 2. The Selecting Committee can defer their decision about any animal and can order it to be set back until the next parade takes place.

Paragraph 10.

1. The Secondary or next Selecting Parade is usually held in April, the place and time of the meeting is settled by the Selecting Committee. The following horses may be brought forward:

1. Those set back by the Selecting Committee at the regular parade (Paragraph 9 § 2.)
2. Any horses for which a Veterinary Certificate can be produced saying they were not in a fit state of health to appear at the regular parade.
3. Any horses imported into the Duchy since the first meeting.

§ 2. The Selecting Committee has the right of ordering other parades to be held after the regular or second ones, these must then take place within three months of the dates of these meetings.

§ 3. The Selecting Committee can order a parade at any time if they are asked to do so by the owner of a stallion on the condition that he bears all the expenses of the parade and deposits a sum, named by the Selecting Committee, for that purpose.

2. Revision Selecting Parades.

Paragraph 11.

§ 1. Every owner of a rejected horse has the right to demand that his animal may be brought before the Revision Committee.

§ 2. The demand for a revision can be made to the Chairman directly after the decisions of the Selecting Committee are made known, must take place however within 8 days, accompanied by a sum of £ 2.10.0, otherwise the right of appeal is disallowed.

§ 3. These appeals are usually settled directly after the Secondary Selecting Parade (Paragraph 10 § 1), the Chairman then calls the Revision Committee together.

The Revision Committee is formed of the three permanent members of the Selecting Committee, the three non-permanent members and their proxies of the district from which the horse in dispute comes.

At least seven members of the Revision Committee must be present, else there is no quorum.

In exceptional cases, the Revision Committee may be called upon to act before the distribution of Premiums. where the owner of a stallion makes an appeal immediately after the decision of the Selecting Committee has become known.

§ 4. The horse in dispute has to be examined by two Veterinary Inspectors appointed by the Ministry of State, Home Department, and the Veterinary Inspector who examined him in the first instance. before the Revision Committee is called upon to act.

The veterinary examination has to take place according to instructions given by the Ministry of State and which have been suggested by the Selecting Committee.

The Selecting Committee has the power to dispense with the second veterinary inspection, if the horse was declared to be sound on his first examination.

§ 5. If the Veterinary Inspectors say they cannot at present determine if the horse is sound or not. the Revision Committee can appoint another time within the next three months for the animal to be examined.

§ 6. The horse must be passed by a two-thirds majority of the Revision Committee, otherwise he cannot be selected.

§ 7. The decision of the Revision Committee is final.

§ 8. If the owner of the horse in dispute does not bring him up before the Revision Committee or fails in his suit, he forfeits the £ 2.10.0 to the Rates; if the horse is selected. his money is paid back.

3. Service Permits, Fees, Lists and Certificates.

Paragraph 12.

The Selecting Committee gives the owner of a selected stallion a service permit available for the season. A fee. suggested by the Selecting Committee and confirmed by the Ministry of State, Home Department. is charged for each permit. the sum thus collected to be used for the benefit of horse breeding in general.

Paragraph 13.

The Ministry of State, Home Department, after consulting the Selecting Committee, who in their turn have heard what the various Breeder's Societies have to say on the subject, fixes the lowest sum allowed to be charged for service fees in the district.

Paragraph 14.

§ 1. The owner of a selected stallion is bound to keep a service record and also a list of mares served for the use of the Stud Book and another for the Ministry of State, Home Department, for statistical purposes.

§ 2. He is also required to give the owner of a mare that has been served a certificate of service. after the fees have been paid.

4. Service of Stallions.

Paragraph 15.

The mares in the district may only be served by the stallion selected for that district, with the exception of those mentioned in Paragraph 8, § 2. A stallion selected for one district can be used on mares in another, if the owner of the stallion asks the permission of the three permanent members of the Selecting Committee and they grant his request.

The Selecting Committee can allow fresh blood to be introduced from studs outside the district or foreign sources if they think the proposed animals for use are true to type and likely to benefit the breed.

The use of stallions standing outside the district can also be allowed by the Selecting Committee, if the mares can be proved to have no Oldenburg blood in their veins for three generations, or for those mares which are not of the Oldenburg type.

The progeny of these mares (see Chapter 3 concerning the use of foreign horses) cannot be entered in the Stud Book.

Paragraph 16.

The owners or keepers of stallions are required to place a black board on the doors of the stables in which the stallions are housed, on which the following particulars have to be given in white lettering and distinct writing:

1. Name of Stallion.
2. Year of birth.
3. Colour and markings, if any.
4. Pedigree.
5. Date of last Service Permit.

Paragraph 17.

Three-year-old colts that have not as yet been before the Selecting Committee or colts of the same age that have been rejected are, from 1st May to 15th July, and older horses from the 1st April to the 15th July, not allowed to occupy the same stable or be kept in the same yard as stallions that have been selected.

B. Premium Awards.

Paragraph 18.

The Ministry of State, Home Department, arranges the number and amount of Premiums which are given yearly for first-class stallions and mares.

Paragraph 19.

§ 1. The premium stallions and mares are branded on the near hip with O. surmounted by a crown.

§ 2. The premium stallions must be kept four years, those that receive earnest or advance money two years following the receipt of the premiums, for service in the district.

§ 3. The owner of a premium or earnest-money horse, who does not fulfil the conditions mentioned in § 2, has to return the money received to the Rates and also pay a fine in the first year of 100 %, second year 75 %, third year 50 %, and fourth year of 25 % of the amount of the premium.

The Ministry of State, Home Department, at the request of the Selecting Committee, can commute the service period of four years to three and can also release from the payment of a forfeit or reduce the amount.

§ 4. The following conditions must be fulfilled by the owner of a premium mare, otherwise he is liable to have to return the premium and also to pay a fine of the like amount.

1. The premium mare must, for the next three years, be covered by a premium stallion or by one approved by the Selecting Committee.

   The Selecting Committee can release an owner from this condition if he can show reasonable grounds, before the season commences, why it should be done.

2. The premium mare must be paraded before the Selecting Committee each year, during the period mentioned in condition 1, at a time and place appointed by it, foals dropped during this period have to be sent with her and the Service Certificate for the year produced.

   The owner of the mare must pay back the premium if he does not send her to the parade, unless he can prove to the Selecting Committee, beyond doubt, that he has a reasonable excuse for not doing so.

Paragraph 20.

§ 1. The Ministry of State, Home Department, can arrange the number and amount of premiums to be given yearly for promising colt and filly foals.

§ 2. The owner of a premium foal is bound to fulfil the following conditions; he must otherwise return the premium and also forfeits a like sum as a fine.

1. The colt foal
   (a) is not allowed to be sold outside the district during the year following that in which it has received the premium,
   (b) to send the foal to the next Show and to accept all further premiums allotted to it,
   (c) if the colt is a two-year-old or as long as it is rising three, when it receives the premium, it must in the next year be paraded before the Selecting Committee and if it is selected it must be kept in the district for service the year following.
2. The filly foal
   (a) must not be sold outside the district till it reaches the breeding age,
   (b) must during this period be sent each year to the parade,
   (c) must be served when it reaches the proper age.

The Selecting Committee has the right to absolve owners from these conditions if they have reasonable grounds for doing so.

C. Trials and Competitions.

Paragraph 21.

The Ministry of State, Home Department, can set aside monies to assist the holding of trials or competitions with the object of increasing the value of the Oldenburg as a coach horse, more especially for really good performances in harness; it can also grant money for prizes.

D. Stud Books.

Paragraph 22.

Each district has its own Stud Book.

The Stud Book for the northern district is for those horses which are of the heavy upstanding Oldenburg coach horse type, that of the southern district for those of the medium weight, stylish, harness horse class.

The Stud Book of the northern division is named

"Oldenburg Stud Book"
(Upstanding Heavy Coach Horse).

that of the southern division,

"South Oldenburg Stud Book"
(Medium Heavy Stylish Harness Horse).

Paragraph 23.

A separate page has to be used in the Stud Book of the northern division for each of the animals mentioned.

1. for all selected stallions,
2. all mares in the district that are descended from a mare already entered, as soon as they are used for breeding; mares that have a dam that is registered, but are sired by a horse outside the district can only be entered after they have passed the Selecting Committee.
3. the owners of three-year-old fillies and older mares who think their horses are true to the coach horse type can have them entered if they pass the Selecting Committee (Paragraph 22). The progeny of a mare that is already entered is in the first instance noted on her page. with the exception of those foals that fall from a mare that has been served by a horse outside her own district (Paragraph 15).

Paragraph 24.

The Pedigree Register issued by the Ministry of State, Home Department, on the 18th March, 1886, and the Stud Book edited by the horse-breeder Eduard Lübben and carried on by the Oldenburg Horse Breeders'

Society as the "Oldenburg Stud Book" (Volumes I. and II.) are a recognised part of the Stud Book for the northern district.

Their value, as a groundwork for the following editions of the Stud Book has been recognised by the Ministry of State, Home Department; the same can be said of documents that have been collected for the use of the "Oldenburg Stud Book" but which are not yet in print.

Paragraph 25.

In the Stud Book of the southern division a separate leaf has to be used for each of the following:

1. all stallions selected for use in the district,
2. (a) all three-year-old fillies in the district that are descended from mares already entered,
   (b) all three-year-old fillies that have been awarded premiums as foals and such fillies that have been bought as foals by the aid of State grants that are still in the district,
   (c) other three-year-old fillies and older mares if the owners wish to have them entered, these must, however, first be passed by the Selecting Committee (Paragraph 22).

Foals, in the first instance, are to be entered on the page set aside for their dams.

Paragraph 26.

The owners of fillies descended from mares registered in the Stud Book are bound to be brought before the Selecting Committee, as soon as they are three years of age, for approval, before they can be entered.

Paragraph 27.

All horses, that have a page of their own in either of the Stud Books and all foals in the northern district that are entered on their dam's page, are branded with the Stud Book mark, except those stallions which have been imported for change of blood and their offspring until they have been selected.

Paragraph 28.

The Ministry of State, Home Department, fixes the fees to be paid for entry in the Stud Book, for certificates, for branding and noting foals on their dam's page; these amounts are paid to the account of the Breeders' Society of the district concerned.

Paragraph 29.

In the northern district, the Secretary of the Breeders' Society. controlled by the Selecting Committee is answerable for all entries made in the Stud Book. The management of the Stud Book in the southern division is undertaken by the Selecting Committee themselves helped by the Secretary of the Society.

Paragraph 30.

Each owner or part-owner of a horse that has a page of its own in Stud Book, is a member of the Society of that district to which the horse belongs.

Paragraph 31.

The rights and privileges of membership cease,

1. when the horse entered passes into other hands and is no longer their property,
2. dies,
3. is sent out of the district for any length of time,
4. cannot be any longer used for breeding purposes,
5. or is not used to breed from for some time, in this latter case, the membership only ceases on a request in writing to the Council of the Breeders' Society and then only at the end of the current year.

Paragraph 32.

To make the work of the Society easier, especially where votes have to be collected, each breeding district is divided up into smaller portions, the boundaries of which are settled by the Ministry of State. Home Department. and which we will call Local Board Districts. The members living in these local districts form the Local Horse Breeders' Society. These Local Societies choose a Chairman. two members to act on the Local Boards and one proxy.

In the northern division the Chairman is their representative at the Council Meetings of the Society. in case he cannot be present one of the other elected members takes his place. the person chosen being nominated by the Local Board.

In the southern district the Chairman and one of the local members are nominated to attend the Council Meetings of the Horse Breeders' Society. the other member and his proxy take the place of the first mentioned two if they are in any way prevented from attending these meetings.

Paragraph 33.

The Breeder's Society is represented through their Council which is formed in the manner mentioned in Paragraph 32.

The management of the Society is undertaken:

1. as regards the general business by a Committee of the Council. this Committee consists of a Chairman and at least two members of the Society and a proxy, they are elected by the Council but the choice has also to be sanctioned by the Ministry of State. Home Department,
2. the local business is settled by the Local Boards.

Paragraph 34.

In case of anyone refusing to act in the capacity for which he is chosen. the penalties mentioned in paragraph 4, § 5 come into force.

Paragraph 35.

The expenditure on management, in so far as it is not met by State grants or from other sources. is covered by subscription from all the members. The Council settles the amount to be paid each year by the members, it is raised in the following manner: The owner of a stallion that has received a premium from the State pays four units. of a selected stallion, three, of a mare that has a State premium, as long as the owner is bound under paragraph 19. § 4, two, of an entered mare one unit.

§ 2. If a member refuses to pay his subscription, it is recovered by the same means as if he refused to pay his taxes.

Paragraph 36.

In the northern district a Secretary is nominated by the Council and engaged by the Ministry of State. Home Department. to keep the Stud Book. He stands under the direct control of the Council. His salary is fixed by the Ministry of State. Home Department, the State pays half of this amount. The Secretary is sworn in, his duties are determined by the Ministry of State. Home Department.

Paragraph 37.

Any other matters concerning arrangement and keeping the Stud Books. the entry of horses or the organisation of the Breeders' Societies are issued by the Ministry of State, Home Department.

The winding up of the Stud Book can be ordered by the Ministry of State after consultation with the Breeders' Society and Selecting Committee.

E. Grants to aid the Purchase of Stallions, Fillies and Filly Foals.

Paragraph 38.

§ 1. The Ministry of State, Home Department, can make grants to the Breeders' Society of the Southern Division, to enable it to buy suitable stallions for the use of its members and can fix the conditions under which the grant is to be made, it can also reserve any premiums, that may not have been allotted, to form a fund for this purpose.

§ 2. A stallion, partly bought by State aid, must not be taken out of the district as long as he remains in use, unless special permission is obtained from the Selecting Committee. If this rule is broken the money granted has to be returned to the State.

Paragraph 39.

§ 1. The Breeders' Societies can also receive grants from the Ministry of State, Home Department, to buy fillies and filly foals, but must abide by the conditions imposed by the State.

§ 2. Each purchaser of a filly foal from the Society is bound:

1. not to sell the animal outside the district till it is three years of age, to feed and care for it well during this time and in case he sells it in the district to inform the Chairman of the Society, within 14 days, of such sale,
2. to send it to the yearly parade,
3. to have the filly served when three years old and to take it before the Selecting Committee to have its entry in the Stud Book approved of.

The Selecting Committee can release the buyer from his obligations under 1 to 3 if the animal does not thrive well or does not come up to the type of the breed.

F. Penalties.

Paragraph 40.

§ 1. Fines up to £ 7.10.0 can be imposed if:

1. any person uses or causes a non-selected stallion to be used for breeding purposes,
2. any person who lets his mare be served by a non-selected horse standing outside the district, or without the permission of the Selecting Committee, by a foreign stallion standing outside the district (paragraph 15),
3. any person who uses a stallion belonging to a syndicate, otherwise than mentioned in paragraph 8, § 2.
4. any person bringing a stallion before the Selecting Committee or a mare for the purpose of entry in the Stud Book, who knowingly gives false information concerning age or pedigree, or who shows false certificates or has made alterations on the same,
5. any person who has bought a filly or filly foal from the Society, if such animal has been partly paid for by a State Grant who does not fulfil the conditions mentioned in paragraph 39, sells it outside the district or does not have it served when it reaches the proper age.

Each case mentioned from 1 to 3 is a separate offence and punishable as such.

If a stallion keeper has two at the same time, one selected and one non-selected and uses the non-selected one on any mares except his own, and if it can be proved that he has done this twice in any one season, the service permit is withdrawn from the selected stallion whether it is his own property or not. Even if he makes a complaint to show reason why the service permit should not be withdrawn it is held in abeyance for the time being.

§ 2. Fines up to £ 7.10.0 are also imposed on:

1. a stallion keeper who accepts a lower service-fee than that arranged by the Ministry of State, Home Department, paragraph 13, or does not keep his books in order, paragraph 14 § 1, or who does not do what is required of him in paragraphs 16 and 17.
2. anyone who sells a filly or filly foal that he has bought from his Society without making the necessary report, paragraph 39
3. anyone who makes or causes false entries to be made in the service book or statistical list (paragraph 14) or who gives or causes to be given to the owner of a mare a Service Certificate containing false statements, is liable to a fine up to £ 50 or to imprisonment up to six months.

Paragraph 41.

The fines threatened in paragraph 40 (§§1 and 2) can, by the law passed on the 25th March, 1879, be settled or remitted by the police.

Paragraph 42.

The Ministry of State, Home Department, uses these fines for the benefit of Horse Breeding in the district from which they come.

G. Final Determinations.

Paragraph 43.

The Ministry of State, Home Department, is the officially recognised power to carry these regulations into effect, except where the law passed on 5th December, 1868, otherwise directs.

Paragraph 44.

All other Regulations for the improvement of horse breeding, prior to this, are now declared void.

Paragraph 45.

The time at which these Regulations come into force will be made known later on.

Appendix A.[*]

Register and summary list of horses presented and saddles, bridles etc., etc., given with them to various persons by the noble Herr Johann, Count in Altenburk and Delmenhorst, Herr of Jever, my honoured master, during the time I, Albert Jüchter, was his Honour's most faithful and humble servant and equerry, year by year and piece by piece as follows:

Anno 1583

April 20th, my right worshipful master presented a horse named The Ovelgunner to the Duke of Pomerania. A bridle and bit was sent with the horse, also a simple headpiece, the last mentioned was taken from the inventory of Jacob Bereiterss.

March 12th, m. r. w. m. presented a horse from the Ovelgönne to the Duke of Mecklenburgk.

May 5th, m. r. w. m. was given a horse, a light brown, by Jeka of Kniphausen, he presented Her Grace with a palfrey from Kalckreuter in return, did not get anything with my horse except bridle, bit and halter.

May 11th, m. r. w. m. gave a horse from the Ovelgönne to Christoffer Kalckreutern, I took bridle, bit and halter from the harness-room here to send with it.

May 28th, m. r. w. m. gave a chestnut palfrey to Ludtken von Königsmarck, my honoured master got this animal from Abraham von Ennigen, Lüdtken was sent the palfrey's bridle, as he always has been ridden in this, a halter and stuff to plait in the mane were sent with it.

July 26th a sorrel horse was sent from the High Bailiff at Lungen to Christoffer Königsmarck, High Bailiff, my honoured master afterwards exchanged this horse with him and gave him a young one instead, which he had taken from Ovelgönne to his estate at Jever.

August 3rd m. r. w. m. presented a horse called the Ovuelgunner to the Bishop of Cologne, Gebharten Truchsess; saddle, bridle and velvet trappings were sent with it, these were given to my honoured master by a Danish Nobleman, Marthes Nahrman, along with a sorrel horse, the Elector of Cologne was also sent the saddle-bags.

August 6th m r.w.m. sent a horse together with saddle, bridle, bridle chains (curb & c.) in fact everything complete to the young Duke of Harborg, the horse's name was Eytell Heindrich.

August 18th. m. r. w. m. had a black horse fetched from Ovelgönne

*) It is impossible to reproduce in English the quaint old German Language of those times, suffice it to say that many words with the same meaning are spelt quite differently although not far apart in the text, I have left those I could as a sample. It is interesting to note how different people were treated in the matter of saddlery and trappings, the Bishops seemingly came off best.

The Translator.

and gave it to Eytell Heindrich together with saddle, bridle and bit, these were taken from the armoury, they had been overhauled by the saddler.

August 26th. m. r. w. m. gave Eytell Heindrich 2 geldings, one came from Blankenburg and the other from Welssborg, the bridles I found in a box, I had reins, cut out of my honoured master's leather. made for them by the saddler, these together with 2 halters were sent with the horses.

Also on his date, m. r. w. m. exchanged a grey nag gelding with the Marshal Albert Lueningk for a brown horse with white hind quarters.

September 7 th. m. r. w. m. presented a chestnut to Duke Moriz of Saxony which had been given him by Frau Freydach. only a halter and bridle was sent with the horse.

October 2nd m. r. w. m. had a black horse fetched from Ovelgönne and sent to Count von Bemhen with halter only.

December 11th m. r. w. m. presented Count Albrecht von Barby with a charger which he bought some time ago at Jever. bridle, bit and halter were sent with the horse, the bridle and bit were taken from the harness room.

December 15th. m. r. w. m. gave a chestnut horse away, it came from the Jade and was sent to Tonniess von Weyhe with halter only.

The grey palfrey from Kalckreuter has been sent to the baptismal festivities at Neuenburg as the young master Tonniss Gunter is to be baptised, after this event my honoured master is going to Sundershausen; at this juncture one of the King of Denmark's grooms came in great haste to Altenburg and wanted to ride after my master without delay, the bailiff ordered the horse to be given to him with saddle, bridle, saddlebags and everything belonging thereto. The groom sold the lot at Oldendorpe.

Anno 1584.

January 7th m. r. w. m. presented a horse called The Puschke to the Count vom Bauchem, velvet trappings and everything else belonging to the same and a couple of saddlebags were sent with it.

January 8th m. r. w. m. presented a young horse brought from Rastede to the Ambassador of the Duke of Pomerania. a new bridle. a travelling saddle and new halter were given as well. The saddler supplied these.

January 8th m. r. w. m. gave a young dark brown horse, called the Ovuelgunner, to the Ambassador from Anhalt. a new bridle and halter and a travelling saddle went with the horse.

The horse that m. r. w. m. got from Lorenz von Hern, he gave to the Ambassador Eyndorf from Nassau. Saddle, bridle and belongings were sent with it.

April 1st m. r. w. m. sent a horse (called Boygingk which had been some time at the Wildens at Witbeckersbourg) to his Majesty the King of Denmark. saddle, saddlebags and all necessary harness were sent with it. it was all taken from the armoury and was sent to Witbeckersborg along with the horse.

April 4th m. r. w. m. went to Jever and took the King's groom Hanss Lymborg with him. a horse was sent to Jever only bridle and bit were sent with it.

May 5th m. r. w. m. gave a horse, which your Honour got from Willem rosen to Count Schomborg at the Court in Cassel, saddle and bridle were sent with it.

May 5th m. r. w. m. gave another horse which had come from Ovelgönne to Count Mansfeldt, a leather halter and wooden bit were sent with it.

May 26th m. r. w. m. gave a horse to Count Herman von Wedde. Your Honour got this horse from the lad

Albert Voss, saddle, bridle and everything proper were sent with it.

June 11th m. r. w. m. presented a horse which your Honour ordered to be bought at the fair to Duke Philipso von Grubenhagen's Duchess. Only a halter was sent with it.

June 22nd m. r. w. m. gave a sorrel horse to Ernst Mülert the High Bailiff at Lingen. Your Honour got this horse from Count Herman von Wedde, reins, bit-bridle and halter were sent with it.

June 23rd m. r. w. m. gave a horse that had come from Jever named Lichthort to Count von Wedde. Saddle, bridle, saddle-bags and halter were sent with it.

June 27th m. r. w. m. sent to Ovelgönne for a young horse direct from the grass and gave it to Count Hans Höyer von Mansfeldt. A leather halter was sent with it.

July 18th m. r. w. m. gave a horse named the Big Kalckreuter to the Bishop of Minden. Saddle, bridle, velvet trappings, saddle-bags, bridle chains, everything that belongs to a rightly caparisoned horse were sent with it. The stirrups were taken from Wulf Wiltschunzen's saddle.

July 23rd. The Countess, my honoured mistress, gave a white palfrey to Lübben at Eyben-on-Sands. This horse came from Franckenhausen. Only a halter was sent with it.

August 16th m. r. w. m. gave a horse to Captain Heindrich vonn Zarenhusen, Frankreich brought it from the Ovelgönne. Only a halter and holsters were sent with it.

August 23rd m. r. w. m. gave a pony to the son of Count Albrecht von Schwarzburg. If I am right the son's name was Carll Gunther; the Bishop of Bremen had given the pony to our little Hans. Only its own bridle and halter were sent with it.

August 31st my honoured mistress received a horse as a present from Balgar von Werden, this my noble Lord gave to Count Anthonius, only halter and bridle were sent with the horse.

November 4th m. r. w. m. sent for a horse named Untreuve from Ovelgönne which my honoured master had got from Almas von Buzwarden. this was given to His Honour Meinert Sparenberger. with saddle, bridle, saddle-bags, bridle chains and all that belongs to a rightly caparisoned horse.

Also Meynert Sparenberg was given for his horse on his departure by my noble lord's commands, saddle, bridle, saddlebags, bridle chains and all that belongs to a rightly caparisoned horse.

November 28th m. r. w. m. gave a horse to the High Bailiff Christopher Königssmarck called the Ovuelgunner. Only a halter was sent with it.

Anno 1585

January 2nd m. r. w. m. sent a brown horse to Wilssborg, the bridle in which he is accustomed to be ridden including reins and bit were sent with it these were taken from the harness room. The horse was afterwards sent from Wilssborg by Kolpin to the Bailiff Heinrich Birkoren with saddle, bridle and everything belonging thereto also old stuff for plaiting in the mane.

January 4th m. r. w. m. gave a horse called the Taschenfeger to Count Eberhart von Mansholt at Arenstein, his own reins and bit, the rest of the bridle being old, also a leather halter were sent with it.

January 17th m. r. w. m. gave a light brown palfrey named Steiter Clauvs to Count Volraden von Valdeck, an old bridle, reins and bit as well as a leather halter were sent with it.

January 18th m. r. w. m. exchanged a horse named Emüger with Otto von Bochmer for a reddish-brown horse, each horse kept his own saddle until further notice, nothing else beside reins, bit and halter were sent with it.

January 19th m. r. w. m. gave a horse that your honour had given you by Boehmers to Johan von Ahlen nothing but a bit with reins, an old headpiece and halter were sent with it.

January 29th m. r. w. m. exchanged horses with Lorenz von Horn your honour sent a brown named Wilssburger and got a black back, each horse retained his own reins, bridle, saddle and halter.

April 3rd m. r. w. m. gave a horse called "The Big Gelding" to the High Bailiff at Jever, Brother Christoffer Böselager, saddle, bit and halter were sent with it.

April 5th m. r. w. m. presented a young horse named the Ovelgönner to Count Hans von Schwarzburgk, a bridle with wooden bit and horse-cloth were sent with it.

April 6th m. r. w. m. gave a horse named the Delmenhorster to Ernst von Mandelsslor, saddle and halter and what belongs to same, were sent with it.

June 6th m. r. w. m. presented a horse to the Bishop of Magdeburg, Markgrave Joachim Fridrich, the Neuenfelder by name, I took reins and a bit from an old bridle which I got from the harness room to send with it.

July 9th m. r. w. m. sent for a chestnut horse from Ovelgönne which was presented with all honours to the Duke Moritz of Saxony, saddle, bridle, velvet trappings were sent with it. The reins and bit were taken from the harness room and were originally bought from a trader that came from Brunswick.

July 14th m. r. w. m. exchanged horses with Duke Moritz, your Honour gave a piebald and got a brown in return, saddles, reins, bits and halters were exchanged with the horses.

On the same day m r. w. m. sent a horse to Blexersande to the Wilden called the Old Chestnut, your Honour got this horse some time back from the Danes.

August 13th m. r. w. m. presented a young horse that your Honour got from Poppe von Stumpenser to Count von Schwarzburgk at Jever.

August 16th m. r. w. m. presented a horse named the Boygingk to the Bishop of Halberstadt and Minden, Duke Heindrich, together with velvet trappings, saddle-bags and all that belongs to a rightly caparisoned horse.

On the same date your honour gave a horse named ...... to Johan von Ussline, High Bailiff at Sernbarg, nothing was sent with the horse but an old headpiece, reins and bit-halter.

August 16th m. r. w. m. presented a horse called Rosstauscher to Count Albrecht von Schwarzburg. An old headpiece, reins, bit, saddle-bags &c. were sent with it.

September 6th m. r. w. m. presented a brown gelding named the Werder to Count Marten von Holstein, saddle, bridle and saddle-bags were sent with it.

September 18th m. r. w. m. gave a horse named "The High Bailiff Königsmarck" to Your Honours' Brother Count Anthoniuss, nothing was sent with it except reins and halter-bit.

October 11th m. r. w. m. gave a horse called the Old Nynhuser to Agathes Norman with saddle, bit, velvet trappings and all that belongs thereto, saddle-bags, bridle-chains, stuff to plait mane and also a halter.

November 16th m. r. w. m. presented a horse called the Brunswicker to the Ambassador from Luneburg, Rudloffen von Bunauven, reins and bit, taken from an old bridle and holsters were given with it.

November 16th m. r. w. m. presented a young horse which had been fetched from Neuenfelde to the Ambassador from Schöneberg, Werporp, reins and bit from an old bridle, a headpiece and also a halter were given with it.

On the same date m. r. w. m. presented a young grey horse that your Honour got from Jacob Sturren to the Ambassador from Honstein, Jürgen von der Heyde, an old bridle with reins and bit as also a halter were given with it.

Anno 1586.

January 25th m. r. w. m. gave a horse that was foaled at Witbeckerssburg but brought from Ovelgönne by Eylert Frankreich, to Christopher Kalkstein who is with Count Anthonius at Court. Frankreich took the horse there.

January 27th m. r. w. m. presented a horse that had been brought here by the groom Clauss to Count von der Lippe, saddle, bridle, velvet trappings, bridle chains, stuff to plait mane and halter were given with it.

February 23rd m. r. w. m. presented a horse to Count Phylips Ernst von Gleichen, this horse was bought some time ago at Jever, saddle and bridle were sent with it, the saddle and item headpiece had formerly belonged to the Kalckreuter, item a leather halter belongs to Jacob Bereidterss accounts.

February 13th m. r. w. m. gave a horse to Panwell schmit, named the Fanenfuerer, saddle, halter bit and all that belongs to a riding horse were given with it.

On the same date m. r. w. m. sent a horse called the Lauenburger which had been a long time at strouwe, to the Wilden at Wittbeckersburg.

April 5th m. r. w. m. presented a young horse called the Ovuelgunner to Count Lutwig von Stolberg, reins, bit, a plain bridle and halter were given with it.

May 4th m. r. w. m. sent a horse that had been a long time at Ströuve called the Kuyphuser to the Wilden at Witbeckerssburg.

May 20th m. r. w. m. presented a horse that was sent from Ovelgönne to Jever to the young Duke of Weymar, a plain bridle, bit and a halter were sent with it.

The same day 2 young horses were bought in the Country and sent to the Duke.

July 2nd m. r. w. m. presented a grey palfrey to the Duke Magnus of Saxony, his saddle bridle and halter were sent with it.

June 17th m. r. w. m. bought a young horse at Jever, it was given to Your Honours Her Brother Count Anthonius, only bridle and halter were sent with it.

August 5th m. r. w. m. presented Duke Magnus of Saxony with a grey horse, with which were given saddle, bridle, a Welsh loin cloth, saddle-bags and holsters.

August 11th m. r. w. m. gave Captain Johanne von Plettenberg a horse, which my honoured master got from von Almer of Buzwarden, with the horse were sent his bit and reins from the old bridle.

August 15th m. r. w. m. presented Count Wilhelm of Nassau with a young horse, called the Ovuelgönner, the gift also included a saddle with velvet trappings and saddle-bags.

September 4th our m. r. w. m. gave each of the grooms a carriage horse, my honoured master had exchanged them with the Duke Magnus of Saxony.

September 18th m. r. w. m. presented Count Phylipss von Hollarp with a horse called the Meyhusern, saddle, bridle, saddle-bags and all that pertains to a horse were given with it.

On the same date m. r. w. m. gave a horse named the Kalkreuter to Colonel Christoffer Iselstein, saddle, bridle, saddle-bags and all things belonging were given with it.

September 21st m. r. w. m. presented Count von Mörss with a horse called "The Bridegroom", a saddle, bridle saddle bags &c. were given with it.

October 4th m. r. w. m. caused a young horse to be fetched from the Jade, which he presented to Johann Harken zur Nygenburg, nothing was sent with it but a leather halter.

October 12th m. r. w. m. had a horse fetched from Ovelgönne which had been kept for a time at Ströuve the same my honoured master presented to Count Berendt von Waldeck, Bishop of Osenbrügge, nothing was sent with it but an old bridle and a halter with bit which were taken from the harness room.

October 13th m. r. w. m. gave a young horse called the Ovelgönner, to Fritz von dem Berge. An old bridle and saddlebags were sent with it, these were taken from the harness room.

Also my honoured master sent a horse to Ovuelgunne. It had become blind, and is called the Jonitter. Marten the groom had ridden it for a long time, it now goes to Ovuelgunne for the carriage.

Anno 1587.

January 9th m. r. w. m. presented a horse to Duke Otto von der Harburg, which my honoured master had from His Honour the Gentleman of the Bedchamber Kerstian von Harlingen, saddle, and bit-halter accompanied it.

February 7th m. r. w. m. gave a horse away. This horse was foaled at the Witbeckersburg. It was sent from Ovelgönne to Jever, and from thence to Altenburg. The same was given to Count Hermann von der Berge, with saddle and bridle.

February 25th m. r. w. m. presented Duke Wilhelm von Luenenborg at Celle with two horses. They were taken to Scholen, my honoured master sent them with the groom Diedrich Spohler, they had nothing sent with them but a halter and bridle, the upper parts of the bridle were made by the harness maker, and the reins and bits were taken from the harness room.

On the same date m. r. w. m. presented a horse to the Countess von der Hoygen with saddle and bridle, this horse my honoured master got from Lorenz von Horne.

May 16th m. r. w. m. sent a horse to the Wilden at Neuenfelde only a halter was sent with it.

June 13th Karltian von Harlingen received a horse from my honoured master, it had velvet saddle, trappings, bridle, saddle-bags, a halter and stuff to plait in the mane. Count von der Lippe gave my honoured master this horse on the occasion of his wedding (1577).

Beside this, Karstian von Harlingen received two young horses from m. r. w. m., they were sent from Ovelgönne to Oldenburg, and had each old bridles, bits, an halter sent with them.

July 9 th m. r. w. m. presented the Countess of Depholt with a carriage horse. This latter came formerly from Ovelgönne, and had only a halter sent with it.

July 15th m. r. w. m. gave Captain Johann von Plettenberg a horse, called Storzenberger. This came from Ovelgönne, bridle bit and plain headpiece and a halter were sent with it.

August 13th m. r. w. m. presented a young horse, which came originally from Ovelgönne to Captain Claus von Zersen, a bridle, bit and halter were sent with it.

September 6th m. r. w. m. presented Duke Morizen of Saxony with a horse, the animal was formerly sent from Ovelgönne to Jever, and had saddle, bridle, halter, and everything necessary for a horse sent with it.

November 3rd m. r. w. m. presented a black horse to the Duke of Pomerania, Prinz Ernst Ludtwigen, this horse was sent to Wolgast it had come from Ovuelgunne.

On the same date m. r. w. m. presented a horse (which was brought from Ovelgönne by way of Huntebrück to Delmenhorst) to the

Pomeranian Master of Ceremonies, Ernst Eyksteden.

September 8th m. r. w. m. presented a horse to the Bishop of Münster, Count of Schaumburg, the the horse was called Neyhuser and had a plain bridle, reins, bit and halter sent with it.

On the Feast of Stephen m. r. w. m. presented a horse called Lauenburger to Duke Hansen of Holstein at Sonderburg, a plain bridle, reins, bit, halter and stuff to plait in the mane were sent with it.

Anno 1588.

January 23rd m. r. w. m. gave a horse to His Honour's brother Count Anthoniuss The horse was called Henen's Foal, a plain bridle, bit and halter were sent with it.

February 15th m. r. w. m. gave a horse to His Honour's sister the Countess von den Hoyge, the horse was given to my honoured master out of the butjenter country and had nothing sent with it but a leather halter.

February 17th m. r. w. m. presented 10 very fine horses to the Prince of Parma, they were sent to Brussell in Brabant, each horse had its own cloth; six bridles and bits a well as ten pairs of new halters were sent with them.

February 23rd m. r. w. m. gave a horse, called Johan Stedingk, away. a halter and wooden bit were sent with it.

March 20th m. r. w. m. gave a horse called Wylstrap to Count von Euerstein at Nyugarten and Nassow, reins, a plain bridle and bit also a halter were sent with it.

April 13th two unbroken horses were presented to the Duchess of Pomerania, two leather halters went with them.

May 26th m. r. w. m. gave a young coach horse to the Duke Moriz von Sachsen, this horse was sent from Jheuer, in the first instance it had come from Ovelgunnė.

July 28th m. r. w. m. presented two horses to the Duke Heindrich of Brunswick, Bishop of Halberstadt, my honoured master gave the one, his Countess the other, nothing but bridles, bits and halters were sent with them.

On the same date m. r. w. m. gave a horse called Schönberg to the Bishop's Page, plain reins, bridle, bit and halter were sent with it.

July 27th m.r.w.m. gave a horse to Hartwich von Bardendorp, the High Bailiff of Delmenhorst, reins and bit were sent with it.

August 9th m. r. w. m. gave a horse to the Count of the Phalz's Ambassador, I do not know his name, this horse was sent to Nygenburg.

October 2nd m. r. w. m. gave a horse called Jaberge to Diedrich von Zarenhusen only reins, bit and halter were sent with it.

October 29th Ottho von Rochmer was given an unbroken mare with foal.

Anno 1589.

January 12th. The Countess of Hennenberg was sent a horse from Ovelgönne, a leather halter and wooden bit went with it.

January 28th m. r. w. m. gave a young horse called the Ovuelgunner to Peter Guldenstern, plain bridle, reins and bit and a halter were sent with it.

February 14th m. r. w. m. gave a horse called Delmenhorst to Count Phylipss Ernst von Gleichen, plain bridle, reins and bit and a halter were sent with it.

On the same date m. r. w. m. gave a horse called Moorienmer to Ludken von Königsmark, reins, bit and halter were sent with it.

February 17th m. r. w. m. gave a horse called Maryenhuser to Christopher Kalkstein, a plain bridle, bit and halter were given with it.

On the same date my honoured mistress the Countess gave a colt and an unbroken horse to Count Albrecht of Maryenhusen.

February m. r. w. m. gave a young horse Nyehuser to Count Wilhelm von Schwarzburgk, only a plain bridle and bit with halter were sent with it.

Also in the month of February m. r. w. m. gave a horse called Oevelgunner to Christopher Schönenfelt at Nygenborch a plain bridle and bit with halter were sent with it.

At the same time m. r. w. m. gave a horse called the Ovelgönner to Reincke Roder at Nygenborch, also a plain bridle, bit and halter.

March 8th m. r. w. m. gave a young horse called Nygenfelder to Count Albrecht von Schwarzburgk. only a halter was sent with it

March 10th m. r. w. m. exchanged horses with the Count Albrecht von Schwarzburgk, a horse called The Light Brown was sent away and my honoured master got a brown palfrey back.

April 9th m. r. w. m. gave a horse called Lorenz to Franz Winterfeld a new bridle, saddle etc. were sent with it.

Appendix B.

The horses marked thus — Your Grace does not wish to be charged to the Rates but to private persons, (at that time some private breeders had to pay contributions in horses, failing this, their money value) as the Master of the Horse informs me.

List of Horses that Your Grace has given way for the benefit of Your Country.

Anno 1648.

1 large brown horse to Landgrave Fritz 60 Thlr. (Thaler, about 3/—)

2— dark brown Stallions to the Representative residing in Hamburg on the 13 July 100 Thlr.

2— dark brown Stallions to the Chancellor of Holstein, von Hatten, at Osnabrück on the 15 July 100 Thlr.

2 mares to Landgrave Fritz von Hessen on 25 July 200 Thlr.

2 horses a dark chestnut, sire Rittberger, and a light chestnut, sire Springer, to the Landgrave von Arch Kayserlichen Obrist on the 31 July 120 Thlr.

1 horse a dark brown, sire, Beleface to the Emperor's Captain of Cavalry Angel on the 31 July 70 Thlr.

7— black horses with blaze to the Emperor's Ambassador Count von Lamberich on the 17.7th 500 Thlr.

2 horses a grey, sire Kranich and a brown, sire The Handsome Trotter, to the Swedish Legate Ochssenstern on the 23.7th 300 Thlr.

6— light brown geldings to the Mayence Chancellor von Reygensperger 300 Thlr.

4 dark brown Stallions to the Swedish Legate's Secretary Hanss-Sohn 200 Thlr.

7 dun-coloured horses with black manes and tails to the Prince of Orange on the 13 8th 1000 Thlr.

2 horses the grey Turk Bussvohle and the white Turk of Raben Haupt to the Duke Christian of Brunswick and Lüneburg on the 26.8th 700 Thlr.

6 grey stallions to the Elector of Brandenburg's High Chamberlain Burgstorff, 600 Thlr.

10— mares to Count von witgenstein 14 December 700 Thlr.

6 light grey stallions to the Landgrave Friedrich of Hessen 26 Decemb. 600 Thlr.

Anno 1649.

9 horses to the Elector of Cologne 6 February, 460 Thlr.

2 horses a black, sire Cölnischen Bereiter, and a dark brown gelding to General Count Löwenhaubt 14 February 460 Thlr.

2 horses to the Swedish General Steinbock 17 Febr. 200 Thlr.

4 horses to the Swedish Commander in Chief Carl Count of the Pfalz 23 Febr. 1000 Thlr.

6 black horses to Count Ernst Lutwich of Nassau 10 March 600 Thlr.
6 Hubero to the Swedish Commander in Chief Carl Count of the Pfalz 18 March 900 Thlr.
6— black horses to Kay von Anefelt 9 May 800 Thlr.
3— horses to the Chancellor of Mayence Reygensperger in April 300 Thlr.
1— horse to the Imperial Colonel Gratz. 120 Thlr.
4— dark brown horses to Herr von Thumbshire, 15 May. 200 Thlr.
7— horses to the Elector of Brandenburg. 13 June 1000 Thlr.
2— horses to the Elector of Brandenburg's High Chamberlain Burgstorff 13 June, 100 Thlr.
1 horse demanded by a Captain of the Wittenberg Regiment as a contribution. 100 Thlr.
6 mares to the Spanish Colonel Count von Ritberg. 23 Novemb. 400 Thlr.
6— cream coloured mares to the King of Denmark. 30. November 1000 Thlr.
6 grey geldings to the old Landgravin of Hesse 28. X.ber 700 Thlr.
6— grey stallions to the Ruling Landgrave Wilhelm. 800 Thlr.

Anno 1650.

2 horses to the French Ambassador Count de Bresi. 200 Thlr.
1 horse to Colonel Count Löwenhaubt 19 April, 100 Thlr.
8 dark brown horses to the Swedish Legate Salvius, 26 26 April, 800 Thlr.
12— mares to Count Curtz 3 June, 1000 Thlr.
7 mares to Count von Trautmannsdorff 3 June, 700 Thlr.
2 horses to Colonel Steinbok. 300 Thlr.
1 dun-coloured horse to the Count of the Pfalz. Commander in Chief, 110 Thlr.
6— dark brown horses to the Field-Marshall Dorstensohn 14 June, 320 Thlr.
1 Hubero Palfrey to the Landgrave Fritz 22 June, 200 Thlr.
2 black geldings to Doctor Hobken 3 July, 130 Thlr.
2 horses to Colonel Motzen in July, 80 Thlr.
3 horses to the Count of the Pfalz. Commander in Chief, 21 August. 800 Thlr.
2 horses to General Field-Marshal Wrangel, 400 Thlr.
2 horses to Landgrave Fritz of Hesse, 300 Thlr.
2 horses to the Swedish Master of Field-Ordnance Wittenberg.
2 horses to Major-General Lune, 21 August, 300 Thlr.
1 horse to the Swedish Quarter-Master General. 110 Thlr.
1 horse to the Imperial Colonel La Cron, 21 August, 110 Thlr.
1 dark brown stallion to the Commanding General Hofmeister, 60 Thlr.
1 dark brown stallion to Lieutenant-General-Field-Marshal Königsmark on the 7. 7ber., 200 Thlr.
6 horses to Her Imperial Highness. 14 8ber., 1800 Thlr.
3 horses to the picolomini, 600 Thrl.
1 horse to Herr von polheim, 150 Thlr.

Suma Sumarum 23 560 Thlr.

Appendix C.

List of Horses presented by Your Grace in the current year of 1652 to Emperors, Kings, Electors and Counts also to notable personages in their Suites.

12 mares to the Swedish Royal Master-of-Horse Hans Wachtmeister, 19 February, 1300 Thlr.

3 horses to Count Witwolff 15 March, 240 Thlr.

2 black horses to the Chamberlain of the Elector of Brandenburg from Schwerin, 6 April, 600 Thlr.

3 horses to the Elector of Brandenburg, 7 April, 900 Thlr.

1 horse to Count von Waldeck at present at the Court in Brandenburg, 7 April, 150 Thlr.

7 horses to the Imperial Privy-Counsellor Bohn. 700 Thlr.

1 horse to the young Count of Fürstenberk, 11 April, 120 Thlr.

3 horses to the Elector of Cologne. 11 April, 350 Thlr.

1 horse to the Landgrave Friedrich of Hesse in May, 200 Thlr.

2 horses to the Bishop of Münster, 30 May, 400 Thlr.

1 horse to Major Fechte, 1 June, 70 Thlr.

1 horse to Colonel Bairmann, 12 July, 50 Thlr.

6 coach-horses to the Elector of Brandenburg, 12 July, 1400 Thlr.

1 horse to Count Moritz of Nassauv, 29 July, 150 Thlr.

6 coach-horses to the Brandenburg Counsellor Klauss, 9 August, 289 Thlr.

1 horse to the Royal Swedish Major-General von der Linde, 12 August, 300 Thlr.

7 coach-horses to the Elector of Celle. 1800 Thlr.

6 coach-horses to the Elector of Trier, 500 Thlr.

3 horses to the Duke of Würtenberg in 8 st., 400 Thlr.

6 horses to the Grand Duke of Florence 26 8 st. 1800 Thlr.

Summa. 11.819 Thlr.

Entry form for Stallion in Stud Book.

No. ....

Name: ______________ foaled:

Colour and Markings:		Premiums won:	
Pedigree:	Sire: Dam:		
Name and address of breeder:			
Name and address of Owner: (Change of ownership and how disposed of.)	Owner:		District No. .... „ No. .... „ No. .... „ No. ....

Remarks:

Entry form for Mare in Stud Book.

No. ....

Name: .... foaled: ....

Colour and Markings:	....	Premiums won:	....
Pedigree:	Sire: .... Dam:		
Name and address of breeder:	....		
Name and address of Owner: (Change of ownership &c.)	Owner: .... District No. .... „ No. .... „ No. .... „ No.		
Remarks:			

Offspring

No.	Sex	Day and Year of birth	Colour and Markings	Sire's Name	Remarks concerning foal (Sale, Premiums won, Selected, &c.)

Formula A. Front Side

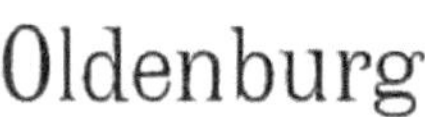

Oldenburg Stud Book

Certificate of Entry

of the Stallion: .... foaled: ....

Colour and Markings: .... Height: .... Cannon-bone: ....

Pedigree:

Sire: ....

Dam: ....

Breeder: ....

Owner and change of ownership: ....

The above mentioned stallion is entered in the Oldenburg Stud Book under the Name and Number given above.

Place and date: .... 19 ......

The Oldenburg Stud Book Society.

For the Council: Stud Book Secretary:

....

Chairman.

Fee 6 M. paid on: ....

The District Chairman:

....

Capabilities see over.

Formula A. Reverse Side

Capabilities.

a) Competitive Trials.

....

....

b) Service Results:

	Number of Mares served in the Year:										Total
Served											
Remained in foal											

c) Description of Offspring,

if they have been honoured by receiving State or Society Premiums or have been Selected as Stallions by the Selecting Committee.

No.	In the Year	Sex	Full Description (Name of Dam, Year of foaling, Premiums won, &c.)	No.	In the Year	Sex	Full Description (Name of Dam, Year of foaling, Premiums won, &c.)

Note: This side of the formula will be filled in by the Selecting Committee when they meet for the purpose of Selecting Stallions at the Yearly Parades.

Formula B. Front Side

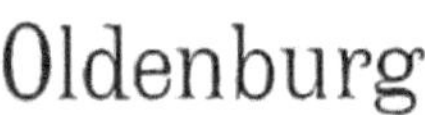

Oldenburg Stud Book

Certificate of Entry

of the Mare: .... No. ....

foaled: .. colour: ....

markings: ....

Pedigree:

Sire: .... No. ....

Dam: No. Sire: .... No. ....

....

....

....

....

Breeder: ....

Owner: ....

The above mentioned mare is entered in the Oldenburg Stud Book under the name and number given above.

Rodenkirchen i. O., the .... 19 ....

The Oldenburg Stud Book Society.

For the Council: Secretary:

....

Chairman.

Fee 3 M. paid on: ....

The District Chairman:

....

Progeny see over.

Formula B. Reverse Side

Register of Progeny.

The mare mentioned on the other side has produced:

No.	Date of Foaling		Sex	Colour and Markings	Name of Sire	Remarks as to what has become of foal, sold, died &c.
	Year	Month and Day				

Formula C. Front Side

Oldenburg Stud Book.

Certificate

of Entry of a Foal as "Offspring" on the Dam's Page.

(§ 5 cipher 45 for carrying out the Regulations under the Law of $\frac{\text{9 April 1897.)}}{\text{4 April 1807.)}}$

We hereby certify that the Member ....

.... of the Oldenburg Horsebreeders' Society has to-day entered under the Dam's No. ....

In the Oldenburg Stud Book of the registered Mare ....

Sire: ....

as Offspring a .... foal

foaled: ....

Colour and markings: ....

Sire of Foal: .... No. ....

Rodenkirchen, ...

Fee paid 1 M.

The District Chairman: Secretary:

....

Formula C. Reverse Side

Notice!

According to § 5 cipher 49 for carrying out the Regulations under the law of $\frac{\text{9 April, 1897}}{\text{4 April, 1907}}$ the Owners of animals entered or announced for entry, are, on the sale of such animals bound to deliver all Certificates of Entry in the Stud Book that are in their hands to the purchaser. If a certificate is lost a duplicate can be obtained from the Chairman of the District on payment of double fees. If it can be proved that the Certificates have been lost under circumstances under which the owner has no control they are then supplied again free of charge. The word "duplicate" must be written across these forms. All other Certificates can be had in duplicate under like conditions.

Under cipher 50 of the Regulations:

> No foal of a registered mare can be sold till it is branded with the Stud Book brand: with the permission of the District Chairman an exception can be made for foals sold within the Breeding District.

Formula D. Front Side

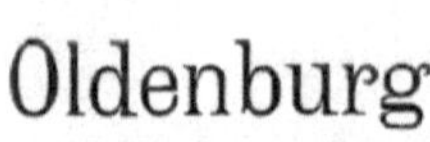

Oldenburg

Stud Book

Certificate.

Pedigree of the $\frac{\text{stallion}}{\text{mare}}$ No. ....

foaled: .... colour and markings: ....

....

Sire:	S.:	S.: .... D.: ....
	D.:	S.: .... D.: ....
Dam:	S.:	S.: .... D.: ....
	D.:	S.: .... D.: ....

Breeder: ....

Owner: ....

Rodenkirchen, the .... 19 ....

The Oldenburg Stud Book Society.

For the Council: Secretary:

....

Chairman.

Fee 2 Mark.

Formula D. Reverse Side

Transfer.

I hereby certify that I have sold the horse mentioned on the other side to

Mr. ....

in ....

....
Signature of Vendor.

.... 19

Formula E.

Oldenburg  Stud Book

Certificate.

The ....

foaled: .... colour: ....

markings: ....

Sire: .... No. ....

is entered on dam's page

....

....

....

....

....

Breeder: ....

Owner: ....

Rodenkirchen, the .... 19 ....

The Oldenburg Stud Book Society.

For the Council: Secretary:

....

Chairman.

Fee 2 Mark.

Formula F. Reverse Side

District No. ……

Foal Formula.

My mare ……

…… Stud Book No. ……

Served by …… No. ……

gave birth to a …… foal

on the ……

Colour and Markings: ……

……

……

Remarks (if barren &c.) ……

……

……

Place and date …… the …… 19

Owners Signature ……

Notice!

Under Paragraph 40 § 3 of the Regulations $\frac{9.\ 4.\ 97}{4.\ 4.\ 07.}$

1. Anyone who makes or causes false entries to be made in the service book or statistical list (paragraph 14) or who gives or causes to be given to the owner of a mare a Service Certificate containing false statements, is liable to a fine up to £ 50 or to imprisonment up to six months.

Formula G. Reverse Side

To be sent to the Chairman latest 15th June.

District No. ……

Notice

of entry for a mare eligible for the Oldenburg Stud Book.

The undersigned announces that his mare

born ……

Colour and Markings ……

Sire …… No. ……

Dam …… No. ……

Name and address of breeder ……

……

Name: …… No. ……
was served by.

Place and date …… the …… 19

……
Owner's Signature.

To be sent to the Secretary in Autumn to enter.

The Chairman of District.

……
Signature

Note of Secretary. The mare mentioned above is entered under No. ……

Name ……

Formula H. Reverse Side

District No. ....

Notice

of sale or change concerning entered animals.

The registered mare ....

.... was ....

sold to ....

....

died from ....
(was slaughtered) ....

Remarks ....

....

....

....

Place and date .... the 19

Owner's Signature ....

Notice!

The sale or death of an entered animal, whether stallion or mare, must be notified to the District Chairman on this form within 14 days, otherwise a fine not exceeding M. 30 will be imposed.

Formula I. Reverse Side

District No. ....

Notice

The undersigned bought from

Vendors { Name: ....
Address: ....

— Stallion — Mare — Foal —

(Here state Name and Number of the animal bought or if entered on dam's page.)

....

....

....

....

....

When bought: .... 19........

Place and date .... the 19

Owner's Signature ....

Notice!

Each purchase of an animal entered or elegible for entry must be notified to the District Chairman within 14 days, otherwise a fine not exceeding M. 30 will be imposed.

Formula K. Reverse Side

District No. ....

Notice.

The Progeny (the .... foal)

of the Mare, Name: ________________ No. ________

foaled 19 ...., served by ....

.... was ....

sold to: ....

died from ....
(was slaughtered) ....

Remarks: ....

....

Place and date .... the 19

Owner's Signature ....

Notice!

Under Paragraph 40 § 3 of the Regulations $\frac{9.\ 4.\ 97}{4.\ 4.\ 07}$

1. Anyone who makes or causes false entries to be made in the service book or statistical list (paragraph 14) or who gives or causes to be given to the owner of a mare a Service Certificate containing false statements, is liable to a fine up to £ 50 or to imprisonment up to six months.

Formula F. G. H. I. K. Front Side

POST CARD.

To

Mr. ....

Chairman of the Oldenburg Horse Breeders' Society

at

____

Post..................................

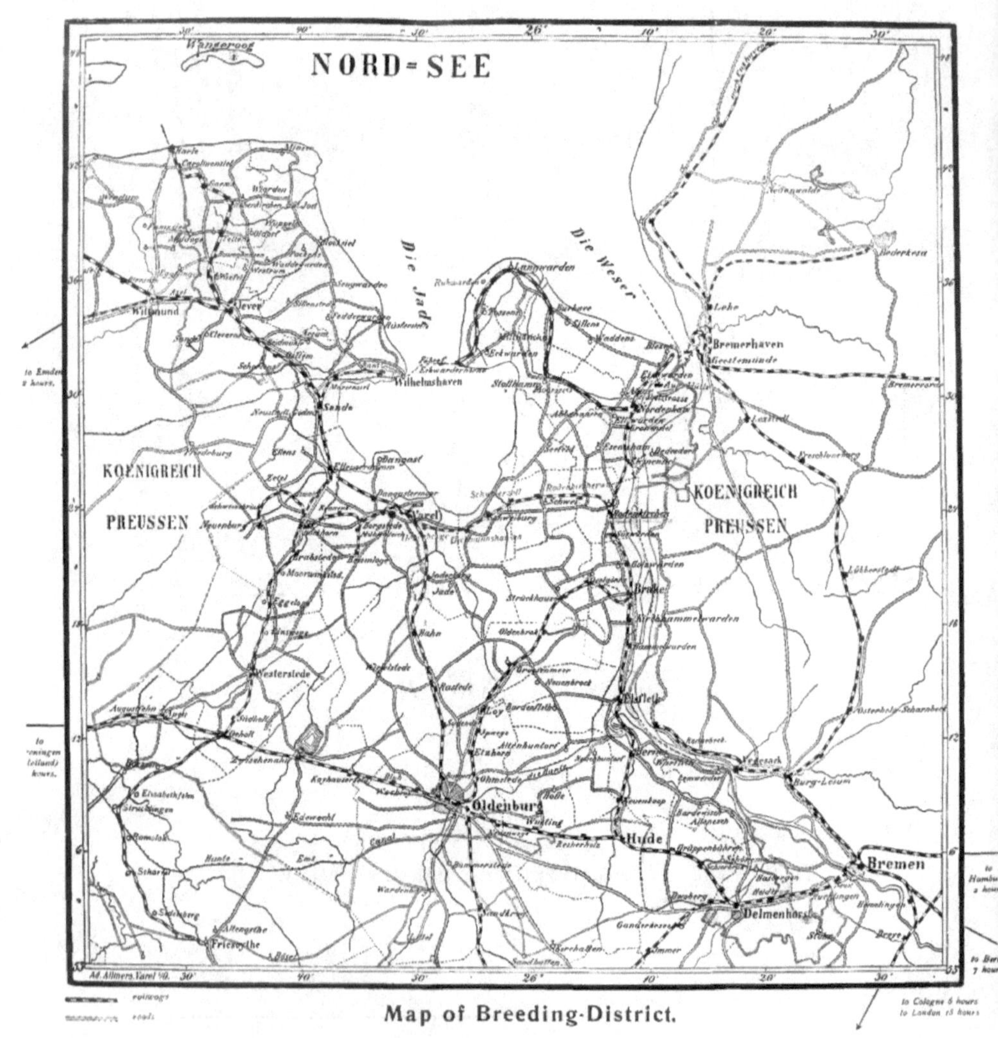

Map of Breeding-District.

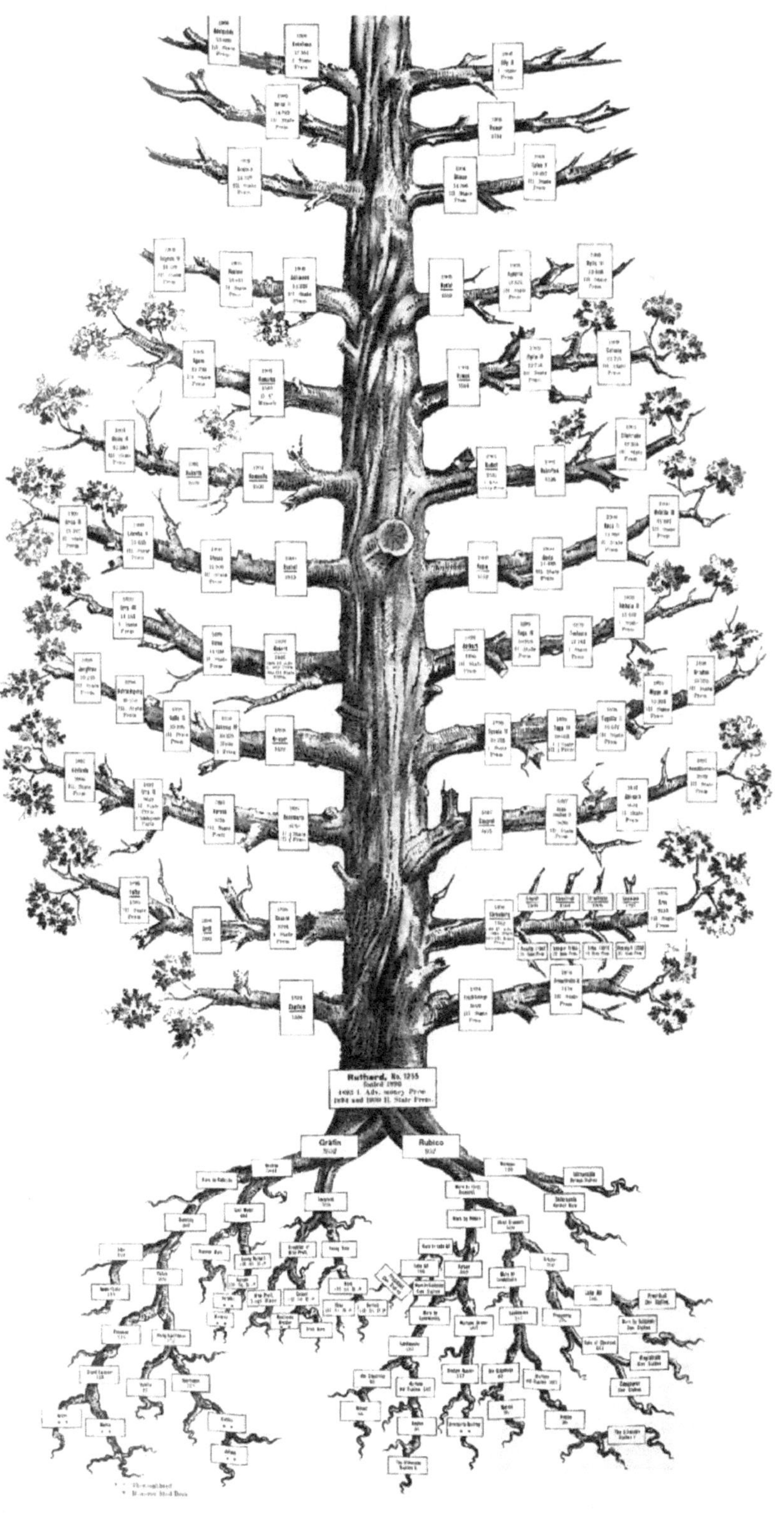
Ruthard, No. 1255
Gräfin
Rubico

Zeitfracht Medien GmbH
Ferdinand-Jühlke-Straße 7
99095 Erfurt, Deutschland
produktsicherheit@kolibri360.de